# From the slave trade
# to 'free' trade:

## How trade undermines
## democracy and justice in Africa

# Fahamu Books

Patrick Burnett & Firoze Manji (eds) (2007) *From the Slave Trade to 'Free' Trade: How Trade Undermines Democracy and Justice in Africa.* Oxford: Fahamu. ISBN: 978-0-9545637-1-4

Issa G. Shivji (2007) *Silences in NGO Discourse: The Role and Future of NGOs in Africa.* Oxford: Fahamu. ISBN: 978-0-9545637-5-2

Firoze Manji & Stephen Marks (eds) (2007) *African Perspectives on China in Africa.* Nairobi and Oxford: Fahamu. ISBN: 978-0-9545637-3-8

Patrick Burnett, Shereen Karmali & Firoze Manji (eds) (2007) *Grace, Tenacity and Eloquence: The Struggle for Women's Rights in Africa.* Nairobi and Oxford: Fahamu & Solidarity for African Women's Rights (SOAWR). ISBN: 978-0-9545637-2-1

Roselynn Musa, Faiza Jama Mohammed & Firoze Manji (eds) (2006) *Breathing Life into the African Union Protocol on Women's Rights in Africa.* Oxford, Nairobi & Addis Ababa: Fahamu, SOAWR and the African Union Commission Directorate of Women, Gender and Development. ISBN: 978-1-94855-66-8

Roselynn Musa, Faiza Jama Mohammed & Firoze Manji (eds) (2006) *Vulgarisation du protocole de l'union africaine sur les droits des femmes en Afrique.* Oxford, Nairobi & Addis Ababa: Fahamu, SOAWR and the African Union Commission Directorate of Women, Gender and Development.
ISBN: 978-1-904855-68-2

Firoze Manji and Patrick Burnett (eds) (2005) *African Voices on Development and Social Justice: Editorials from Pambazuka News 2004.* Dar es Salaam: Mkuki na Nyota Publishers. ISBN: 978-9987-417-35-3

# From the slave trade
# to 'free' trade:

## How trade undermines
## democracy and justice in Africa

Edited by
Patrick Burnett & Firoze Manji

PAMBAZUKA

First published 2007 by Fahamu – Networks for Social Justice
Nairobi & Oxford
www.fahamu.org
www.pambazuka.org

Fahamu, 2nd floor, 51 Cornmarket Street, Oxford OX1 3HA, UK

Fahamu Kenya, PO Box 47158, 00100 GPO, Nairobi, Kenya

British Library Cataloguing in Publication Data
A catalogue record for this book is available from the British Library

ISBN: 978-0-9545637-1-4

Cover illustration and design by Judith Charlton, Fahamu
Manufactured on demand by Lightning Source

This publication was made possible by a grant from HIVOS, www.hivos.nl

# CONTENTS

Introduction
*Firoze Manji and Patrick Burnett*                                        1

About the contributors                                                     5


## TRADE, INVESTMENT AND THE INTERNATIONAL INSTITUTIONS

Plugging the leaks – the role of debt, aid and trade
*Charles Abugre*                                                          10

For life or profit? GATS and the externalisation of Africa's resources
*Oduor Ongwen*                                                            19

Preserving disorder – IMF policies and Kenya's healthcare crisis
*Soren Ambrose*                                                           27

The new scramble for Africa's resources
*Henning Melber*                                                          37

China in Africa
*Stephen Marks*                                                           45

South Africa's Coega complex – cheap energy for industry
*Patrick Bond*                                                            58


## LESSONS FROM THE SLAVE TRADE

A story of the Atlantic slave trade
*Manu Herbstein*                                                          68

Slavery ain't dead, it's manufactured in Liberia's rubber
*Robtel Neajai Pailey*                                                    77

Trade, justice and the case for reparations
*M.P. Giyose*                                                             84


## WOMEN AND TRADE

What do women want?
*Pambazuka News*                                                          90

World trade liberalisation in Africa –
why women are most affected by poverty
*Cheikh Tidiane Dièye*                                                    92

Trade, gender and the search for alternatives –
trade liberalisation and social development
*Jennifer Chiriga*                                                        99

Women and globalisation – the impact on their health
*Mouhamadou Tidiane Kasse* 106

What do women stand to gain from trade? –
women in business and commerce
*Salma Maoulidi* 113

Street vendors and informal trading –
the struggle for the right to trade
*Winnie Mitullah* 119

Friend or foe – the EPAs unmasked
*Liepollo Lebohang Pheko* 125

## TRADE, ENVIRONMENT AND AGRICULTURE

Trade and human rights in the Niger Delta
*Nnimmo Bassey* 136

Community rights and foreign direct investment
in Kenya's Yala Swamp
*Patrick Ochieng* 141

Trading food rights and GM crops
*Interview with Mariam Mayet* 145

International trade (in)justice or the survival of the fattest –
the effects of agricultural subsidies
*Tope Akinwande* 150

Sacrificing the right to food on the altar of free trade
*Jagjit Plahe* 156

Europe – the 'promised land' for Africa's unemployed
*Tope Akinwande* 164

## BOXES

Cocoa trade and children 24

Quick facts on trade 26

The fight for water in Ghana 36

Export processing zones in Kenya 43

Soweto fights for electricity 54

Stop economic partnership agreements 64

Kenya: women workers turn to flower power 103

Facts and figures: women's rights and trade 131

Toxic waste in Africa 147

# INTRODUCTION

### FIROZE MANJI AND PATRICK BURNETT

So, can trade in the era of globalisation be 'just'? Leading up to the 200th commemoration of the abolition of the slave trade and the 50th anniversary of independence in Ghana – both crucial points in marking Africa's historical relationship to the rest of the world – the award-winning weekly electronic newsletter Pambazuka News carried a series of four special issues during 2006 and 2007 that included articles designed to raise awareness and debate on issues of trade and justice. These and other articles from Pambazuka News have been gathered together in this book.

We have chosen a deliberately provocative subtitle for this book: 'how trade undermines democracy and justice in Africa'. In the global trading system, justice and the interests of ordinary working people often take backstage to trade policies dictated by global powers; countries and even entire continents like Africa, frequently appear to be on the losing end of the equation. It is in this context that 2005 saw a cacophony of calls for 'trade justice', defined as a commitment to lobbying for the introduction and implementation of trade rules that work for all people, instead of benefiting those who already have the most.[1] Campaigners for trade justice argued that existing trade rules were damaging to many people, especially the poor and vulnerable, the environment and social policies. They maintained that the global trading system should be rebalanced, taking into account the needs of the poor, human rights, and the environment. But can trade in the era of globalisation be 'just'?

There is much romance about the nature of trade. Trade may not be quite as 'old as the hills', but it has certainly been around since the early emergence of human societies. In its early forms, trade involved exchanges of goods on the basis that there was some equivalence in the amount of time and human labour embodied in the goods. If it took you three days to make a basket, you'd hardly exchange it for something that took much less time to make. But once the class of traders emerged and those who produced were unable to assess the labour equivalence of a commodity, then trade became something different: for the trader's task was to buy below value, and sell above, and the larger the difference between the two, the greater his (and it was usually a 'he') profits. The mercantile cities of Zimbabwe, Timbuktu, Cairo, Venice, etc, all owed their wealth to this form of accumulation. But things have come a long way since then. The 'trade' in African slaves was just the beginning of a major transformation of the nature of trade, leading to an accumulation of capital that fuelled not only the industrial revolution in Europe, but also provided the impetus to the imperial scramble for territory worldwide.

The world market as we know it today has long been conquered, controlled and dominated by metropolitan capital. This was not achieved by economic means alone, but also – and primarily – by the use of brutal force. The metropolitan countries imposed unequal treaties, demolished existing manufacturing industries, enslaved, robbed, seized by tricks, exploited, and carried out wholesale colonisation. Once the conquest of the world market had been achieved, and the North had ensured its domination, and only once that had been guaranteed, did the dogma of 'free trade' get imposed on a world scale. Just as the industrial revolution led to massive over-production and the voracious appetite to conquer the world and seize its markets, so the more recent revolutions in micro- and bio-technology have led, in their own way, to an era of conquering the world through a massive restructuring of economies – which was what the period of structural adjustment programmes and poverty reduc-tion strategy papers was all about.

And it is no surprise that 'free trade' is once again the banner of the neoliberals and neocons. This new voracious surge is what is currently referred to as 'globalisation'. It is what has led to the rich getting richer, and the poor poorer. It is what has condemned us to be consumers, not citizens, and commercially degraded every aspect of our lives. And since only a minority have the capacity to consume, the vast majority of Africa's people are effectively disenfranchised.

And it was precisely the imposition of the neoliberal economic policies that led to the enforced opening of Africa's economies to the free movement of capital – the so-called 'liberalisation' of the market. And once the markets were opened up, one should hardly be surprised that capital in all its forms should seek opportunities in Africa. The penetration of Asian capital – including China, India, Malaysia – as well as from Latin America that we have witnessed recently were only possible once the international financial institutions had been victorious in forcing open African econo-mies to 'free trade'. As Arundhati Roy writes:

There is a notion gaining credence that the free market breaks down national bar-riers, and that corporate globalisation's ultimate destination is a hippie paradise … What the free market undermines is not national sovereignty, but democracy. As the disparity between rich and poor grows, the hidden fist has its work cut out for it. Multinational corporations on the prowl for sweetheart deals that yield enormous profits cannot push through those deals and administer those projects in developing countries without the active connivance of state machinery – the police, the courts, sometimes even the army.[2]

Trade in the era of globalisation is neither 'free' nor 'just'. Behind the arrangements of the world trade system lies the ever present threat of force. As Thomas Friedman put it: 'The hidden hand of the market will never work without a hidden fist. McDonald's cannot flourish without McDonnell Douglas ... And the hidden fist that keeps the world safe for Silicon Valley's technologies to flourish is called the US Army, Air Force, Navy, and Marine Corps.'[3]

The mobilisation for 'fair' or 'just' trade during 2005 received few, if any, concessions, although it was noted that the issues were at least given a higher profile in the minds of many. But as the memory of 2005 faded, it became even more crucial to raise awareness about trade and to encourage debate in this area, especially with 2007 representing the historic milestones of Ghana's 50th independence and the 200th anniversary of the abolition of the slave trade, taking place at a time when new and potentially more onerous trade deals threaten Africa's future development.

This book begins by looking back at 2005 – the year of action for Africa on debt, aid and trade – and what it achieved. This first section considers the role of foreign investment in Africa and the impact of the global financial and trading regime on communities. Why is China so keen to invest in Africa? Why do global trade policies determine the healthcare available to millions of Kenyans? Why is South African industry getting cheaper electricity than poor consumers?

The next section examines diverse issues related to slavery, colonialism and reparations and is followed by an exploration of trade and women's rights. The articles profile the damaging effect of trade policies on the rights of informal traders, who in Africa are often women, how global trade policies have resulted in the feminisation of poverty and how it is the women who have to step in when the state cuts back on health and social services.

The final section deals with agriculture and the environment. Why does the oil trade wreak havoc in the Niger Delta? Why are local communities excluded from development projects driven by multinational companies? Why is it that cotton farmers in West Africa suffer because of a grossly unfair subsidy racket? Why are international trade rules more important than a population's right to food security?

Taken together, these articles provide an insight into how ill-considered trade policies have a profoundly negative impact on the rights of communities. Whether it is the absence of women's voices at global trade negotiations, the decimation of country health systems as a result of international trade policies or the sacrificing of community rights in the interests of multi-national corporations, it is clear that trade polices impose a profit first and people last regime on Africa.

All these articles are also available on the Pambazuka News website at http://www. pambazuka.org/en, where there is a comment facility, enabling readers to add their own views to the debate. The Pambazuka News web page also features recorded interviews, poetry and performances with a general theme of trade and justice. Visit http://www.pambazuka.org/en/broadcasts/index.php to listen to or download these broadcasts. Many of these articles have also been published in the French edition of Pambazuka News, either in their original French versions or in translated form. They can be read at http://www.pambazuka.org/fr.

We acknowledge with thanks the support of HIVOS for the production of these special issues of Pambazuka News and associated podcasts.

**Notes**

1 See <http://www.tjm.org.uk/about/statement.shtml>.

2 Arundhati Roy (2004) *The Ordinary Person's Guide to Empire*. Harper Perennial, p. 37.

3 Thomas L Friedman (1999) *The Lexus and the Olive Tree: Understanding Globalization*. New York: Farrar, Strauss and Giroux, p. 373.

# ABOUT THE CONTRIBUTORS

**Charles Abugre** is currently the head of policy and advocacy at Christian Aid. He has been a development activist in Ghana and many parts of Africa and Asia.

**Tope Akinwande** is a desk officer at the West Africa department of TEARFUND, a leading UK relief and development NGO working in partnership with Christian agencies and churches in over 70 countries to tackle the causes and effects of poverty. His views do not necessarily reflect those of TEARFUND.

**Soren Ambrose** is coordinator of the Solidarity Africa Network, Nairobi, Kenya. He is also associated with the Washington-based 50 Years Is Enough Network, which is involved in an international campaign to shrink or eliminate the IMF.

**Nnimmo Bassey** is executive director of Environmental Rights Action and Friends of the Earth Africa campaign coordinator.

**Patrick Bond** is director of the Centre for Civil Society at the University of KwaZulu-Natal in Durban.

**Patrick Burnett** was the online news editor at Pambazuka News. He has researched, written and edited several Fahamu books and is currently editorial advisor for Pambazuka News.

**Jennifer Chiriga** is unit coordinator, Globalisation and Alternatives Unit, Alternative Information and Development Centre (AIDC), Cape Town.

**Cheikh Tidiane Dieye** is a socio-anthropologist who has been involved in trade and multilateral negotiations on behalf of Enda Tiers-monde, a member of the Africa Trade Network (ATN). He is co-editor of 'Footbridges between trade and durable development', a news bulletin on the trade negotiations.

**M.P. Giyose** is chairman of Jubilee South Africa.

**Manu Herbstein** is a citizen of both South Africa and Ghana. He has lived in Accra since 1970.

**Mouhamadou Tidiane Kasse** is coordinator of *Flamme d'Afrique*, a daily newspaper published by IPAO (the Panos West Africa Institute) and ENDA Third World at meetings of social movements.

**Firoze Manji** is founder and executive director of Fahamu and editor of Pambazuka News.

**Stephen Marks** is a freelance researcher, writer and consultant specialising in issues of economic development, human rights, planning, and the environment.

**Salma Maoulidi** is the executive director of the Sahiba's Sisters Foundation, a women's development network in Tanzania whose mission is to build women's leadership and organisational capacity.

**Mariam Mayet** is with the African Centre for Biodiversity.

**Henning Melber** is executive director of the Dag Hammarskjöld Foundation in Uppsala, Sweden. He has been research director of the Nordic Africa Institute (2000–06) and director of the Namibian Economic Policy Research Unit (NEPRU) in Windhoek (1992–2000).

**Dr Winnie Mitullah** is senior research fellow at the Institute for Development Studies (IDS) at the University of Nairobi.

**Patrick Ochieng** is the founder and executive director of the Ujamaa Centre, which was set up in 2001 as a direct response to the continuing exploitation and exclusion of the coastal peoples of Kenya over the last 40 years. Ujamaa is a key member of the Friends of Yala Swamp.

**Oduor Ongwen** is the country director of the Southern and Eastern Africa Trade Information and Negotiations Institute (SEATINI) in Kenya. Previously, he was the executive director of EcoNews Africa and chaired the National Council of NGOs in Kenya. He holds a master's degree in the economic policy of developing countries.

**Robtel Neajai Pailey** is a native Liberian. She is a postgraduate student at Oxford University, and a multi-media producer for Fahamu and Pambazuka News.

**Liepollo Lebohang Pheko** is a member of the Secretariat for the Gender & Trade Network in Africa, based in Johannesburg.

**Jagjit Plahe** is an activist and academic currently based at Monash University in Melbourne where she coordinates that International Trade Policy Unit. Formerly, Jagjit worked with EcoNews Africa based in Nairobi where she was actively involved in initiating the debt cancellation movement. She is the author of *Multilateral Agreement on Investment: National Sovereignty for Sale?*

Trade, investment and
the international institutions

# PLUGGING THE LEAKS –
# THE ROLE OF DEBT, AID AND TRADE

## CHARLES ABUGRE

February 2006

2005 was supposed to be a year of action for Africa, with demands for 'more and better aid, debt cancellation and more just trade policies'. What happened? Charles Abugre from Christian Aid offers some insights into the demands of the last year and provides pointers on where African civil society should focus its energies in the related areas of aid, debt and trade.

The rationale behind the 'more and better aid, debt cancellation and more just trade policies' is that these will create the conditions to ensure adequate resources to finance Africa's development. Undoubtedly, if fully addressed, these will put more money in the hands of governments and people and ease the resource constraint. I will argue, however, that on their own – never mind the quality of aid, the speed of debt cancellation, the degree of market opening in the North and the end of export subsidies – these demands will not provide the resources adequate for Africa's development.

These demands, though relevant, are slightly misplaced in their singular focus on sources of 'inflows', to the total denial of the mechanisms of 'outflows'. It is the balance of inflows and outflows that creates the net resources for development. I will also argue that the singular focus on 'inflows' entrenches the sense of Africa's dependence and perpetuates the myth of Africa's resource poverty and powerlessness. In addition, in focusing on trade policy to the exclusion of what underlies trade, we miss a fundamental explanation for governments' insistence on liberalisation – beyond the view that they are reckless, ignorant, powerless or uncaring.

## More and better aid

Our demand that governments in the North fulfil their obligation to deliver 0.7 per cent of their gross national product for international development is right. Indeed, it is particularly a right of African countries to demand it, given that this promise has been used repeatedly in the past as a bait to secure economic and social reforms in Africa. But realistically, we know it will not be delivered. The slow pace and low volume of aid increases committed at the 2005 G8 meeting in spite of all the noise – and the subsequent threat by the US to undermine the 0.7 per cent target itself – shows how difficult and risky it is to rely on increasing volumes of aid for Africa's development. The explanation is simple, to the extent that traditional aid continues to depend on taxpayers in the North, its ebbs and flows will depend on the political temperature and economic performance in the North, especially Europe.

But the key problems of aid are its purpose, its governance and its impact on the psychology and accountability of our governments and elites. Official development aid is hardly ever completely altruistic, or single-purpose, or completely divorced from foreign policy. Consequently, we are constantly having to oppose one thing or the other to do with the provision of aid, e.g. tied aid, policy conditioning, human rights conditioning, policy leveraging and more recently the increasing link with the war on terror.

Regardless of the rhetoric, aid cannot be separated from foreign policy objectives and to the extent that these shift, the purpose of aid will shift. And why not? Why shouldn't taxpayers in the North demand that their taxes serve values and goals they hold dear? Why shouldn't they expect their governments to account for the impact of aid, and therefore put in place measures to ensure that their money delivers the purpose for which it is given.

Conditionality is an important issue for Africa largely because aid forms too large a share of budgets. As a result, the risks associated with aid policy are more significant for Africa than in other continents where aid forms a minuscule proportion of budgets. Whilst it is proper to keep ensuring that the conditions associated with the provision and management of aid do not exacerbate Africa's development problems, the real challenge is to reduce aid's importance to Africa's development.

The more debilitating impact of development aid is what it does to the mentality of the African elite and to the processes of democratisation and accountable governance. Governments have developed the myth that their economies cannot survive without aid. In reality, it is their governments and the patronage systems that maintain them which are under threat without the aid machinery.

The competition among African governments for inclusion in the club of favoured nations leads to wilful abandonment – to donors – of sovereignty won at the cost of lives in the anti-colonial struggle. The multi-donor budget support arrangement is one manifestation of this loss of sovereignty. Without a break in the aid dependency mentality, Africa stands no chance of building democracy based on accountability to citizens. Worse still, the imagery that aid agencies – private and official – find necessary to deploy in order to sustain domestic political interest in aid is often an affront to the African personality and spirit, diminishes African self-worth and perpetuates negative stereotypes. Whilst we cannot ignore aid, we should not be glorifying it.

Sometimes we in civil society contribute unconsciously to the erosion of sovereignty and the loss of self-worth. We are sometimes quick to demand or endorse 'governance conditionality' where aid and debt relief are made conditional on progress in these areas. To monitor compliance often requires even greater involvement and power for donors in domestic governance. It is like saying that new forms of colonisation are acceptable on human rights grounds. This is dangerous. Yet there are cases where human rights abuses, dictatorship and corruption are at such a level that the impact of debt relief and aid will be to strengthen repression and enrich a few rather than promote development. What do we do in this situation?

A solution could be based on the principle that regional political bodies are better placed to manage political problems in member states. This is the principle applied by the Economic Community of West African States (ECOWAS), the Southern African Development Community (SADC) and the Africa Union (AU) in conflict resolution and peace building/keeping. This is also the principle underlying the African Peer Review Mechanism (APRM). We propose a peer trust fund to be managed by the AU and used as the financial muscle behind the APRM. Debt relief and humanitarian funds meant for countries abusing their citizens will be paid into this fund, to be held in trust for the country and be released by the AU as the country makes progress in the governance areas of concern. Such a mechanism will:

- Strengthen and give teeth to the AU's desire and capacity to promote accountable and democratic governance in the region
- Act as a muscle and an incentive for the APRM
- Take away the excuse of creditors not to write off debts owed by Africa or withold aid needed for humanitarian purposes but which, for reasons outlined above, cannot be channelled directly to an abusing country or to NGOs
- Allow Africans and their political institutions to drive their own political reforms
- End the arbitrary and selective means by which donors apply governance conditionality.

So what do we need to do about aid? We should:

- Support our Northern partners' efforts to make their governments fulfil their part of the global compact but scale down its importance in Africa's plan of action
- Support the establishment of a peer trust fund to assist the AU to deal with the governance issue
- Increase domestic civil society organisation (CSO) interests and involvement in budget processes so as to reduce the influence of donors on budget governance and steer budgets to deliver public services and fight corruption
- Oppose donor-driven budget management arrangements that undermine

parliamentary oversight and propose parliamentary oversight procedures that are transparent and inclusive of civil society.

Whilst these actions are necessary to improve the quality of aid and reduce its damage, they do not address the resource deficit problem itself.

## Debt

The issue of debt is not so much what we demand but whom we address with what messages. First the message of ending the debt burden has been directed largely in one direction – the creditors. The message itself has been one of appealing for understand- ing whether based on justice or empathy. There is nothing wrong with this in as far as this appeal is coming from our Northern partners and is directed at their publics and governments. Whatever strategies they find feasible for exerting pressure for action should be welcomed by us as long us these strategies neither diminish African dignity nor undermine the messages coming from Africans.

But directing our energies at appealing to Northern creditors suggests our lack of belief in the power of the debtor. However, the Nigerian debt relief effort – no matter how unsatisfactory – and the Argentinean debt restructuring initiative suggest that debtors do have power and can force change. In the Nigerian case, it was the threat by parliament to withhold appropriation for debt servicing and the subsequent road show that the joint committees of parliament undertook in Europe and the US to drum home their threat that forced the Paris Club to rush through a debt relief package. In Argentina's case, an economic and political meltdown, resulting from years of faithful compliance with the International Monetary Fund's (IMF) conditions and faithful debt servicing, forced Argentina to impose a unilateral moratorium on debt servicing and then subsequently unilaterally discounted its debt instruments by 75 per cent. After heaving and puffing, both the IMF and the private creditors accepted their lot and Argentina's economy rebounded.

Africa's debt overhang of over $200 billion provides the muscle for a successful col- lective African threat.  This is the task for the AU and we should make that forcefully clear. The cancellation of $200 billion poses no threat to the global financial system but can save millions of lives. Even a threat of a collective moratorium will send the message clear and loud, especially if this threat were accompanied by an enforceable commitment to transparency and anti-corruption and the channelling of the money so saved into revamping public services. We should not celebrate divisive debt relief initiatives like the one delivered at Gleneagles, although we can celebrate the victory in terms of the comprehensive principle, that is that all debts, including the debt stock owed to the international financial institutions (IFIs), must be cancelled.

So where do we go from here in relation to debt? We should:

- Welcome the principle of debt stock cancellation agreed at Gleneagles and at the annual meeting of the IMF/World Bank but condemn the selectivity and divisive approach
- Develop a strategy to pressurise the AU and its member states to adopt a debtor-led strategy
- Campaign for an international law to regulate international debt.

## Trade

The trade policy focus has been in four areas:

- Defending our domestic markets from further harmful liberalisation
- Defending our producers – especially our farmers – from demise as a result of the dumping of subsidised imports
- Seeking market access without reciprocal market opening obligations
- Promoting regional integration.

These demands are relevant and we should continue to maintain a focus on them. We should prioritise, in particular:

**The defensive interests of our people** For example, our focus on agriculture should be driven by food security and rural development objectives rather than export promotion. Not only is the latter not realistically attainable in a significant way (except traditional commodities), it also detracts from what Africa's needs are at this moment. In this sense, the key policy focus is to prevent any further market opening (liberalisation), whether this is through aid and debt deals or through multilateral negotiations. Better still, the goal should be to protect the space for flexible policy whereby countries can vary tariff policy to meet development goals, starting with consumer goods and shifting to intermediary inputs of capital goods – whilst relaxing consumer good imports – as the economy develops. It is this flexible and progressive use of tariffs that is essential as an industrialisation strategy.

**Conditions for industrialisation** This intersects with the defensive interest. The key constraining factor for industrialisation is demand – the competition from foreign consumer goods which makes it impossible for local producers to carry on producing let alone innovate. Investments in infrastructure including roads and energy will contribute to reducing transaction costs but are not the most constraining to industrialisation. We should not be detracted by the so-called supply-side argument that suggests that investments in infrastructure will correct for competitive pressures. The policy demand is to not give any more market access through the Non-Agricultural Market Access (NAMA) negotiations and others whilst securing the policy space necessary to allow for flexible use of trade policy.

**Defend public services** The aggressive push embarked on by the European Union (EU) and the US at the ongoing talks to open up the services sector reflects the shift in the structure of these economies into services. It also reflects the increasing importance of services for profits and services as a means of gaining control of scarce natural resources such as water. Without the universal provision of public services by the public sector, Africa stands no chance of reducing poverty, managing inequality and conflict and growing the labour force of the future. We should put in all the energy we can marshal to campaign for the universal provision of public services by the public sector, the minimisation of commercial ethos in basic services and the avoidance of market opening commitments.

**Regional markets** The key issue here is to support the AU and sub-regional trading blocks to resist the pressure to make market opening and third-party tariff concessions before the dynamics of intra-regional trade are worked out, not least in the Singapore issues. This suggests the need to postpone the market access aspects of the economic partnership agreements (EPAs) with the EU and to shift energy into campaigning for a

---

*the reality of Africa is that the resources that leak out far exceed those that flow in. This is why Africa is a net exporter of capital. And the sums are staggering.*

---

reform of Article 24 of the Regional Trade Agreements component of the World Trade Organisation (WTO) in order to protect the principle of less than full reciprocity. In the interim we should back the call by the campaign to Stop EPAs for a reform of the rules of origin aspects of the 'Everything But Arms' proposal to make it meaningful for African less developed countries (LDCs).

**The mandate of the WTO and dispute settlement** Developing countries, and Africa in particular, stand to lose with a WTO saddled with a broad rather than a narrow agenda. This is because Africa has the least capacity to defend, let alone promote its interest in multiple negotiating forums. The continent's heavy dependency on the IFIs for resources exposes it to unilateral liberalisation pressures. Once unilateral liberalisation has been embarked upon, there is always the risk of easily committing liberalised sectors to the lock-in mechanism of the WTO. In addition, making commitments on several fronts imposes an implementation burden, the cost of which is relatively higher for poorer countries than richer ones. It is therefore in the interest of Africa to see a slimmer WTO.

However, the decision to focus on trade to the exclusion of investments is a serious limitation. In the first place, the Services Agreement and the Singapore agenda are essentially about investment. It is important to note also that underlying the market access concessions that African governments give to the North, especially in services, is an expectation of foreign direct investment (FDI) and its mythical value as the solution to underdevelopment. Similarly, FDI expectations underlie the anti-inflationary macroeconomic policies of governments and debt servicing compliance.

The belief in FDI is so strong that governments have happily adopted negative taxation policies to attract foreign companies. To have a chance of developing trade and macroeconomic policies that promote development, restrain our governments from giving away market access concessions recklessly and channel attention towards domestic resources for investments, we must first effectively champion more realistic and less jingoistic expectations associated with FDI.

So what do we do in relation to trade and investment? We must:

- Encourage national governments to be more proactive in protecting their markets especially in the area of consumer goods, agriculture and essential public services They will not necessarily suffer punitive action. Even if they do, their economies may still come out better-off
- Drum home to national governments that opening markets will not necessarily bring FDI and even if it does, FDI will not necessarily bring about development
- Encourage the AU to promote a critical debate on the role of FDI in Africa's development
- Continue the campaign for policy flexibility and an end to coerced liberalisation. This is crucial for defending Africa's producers
- Scale down the export focus of agriculture (market access in the north) and emphasise its food security and rural development objectives
- Support the Stop EPAs campaign.

## Financing development: beyond aid, debt relief and trade

What matters for ensuring that governments have adequate resources to finance development are net flows. This means factoring in not just inflows such as earnings from trade, or aid or remittances but also what is lost to the rest if the world. Debt servicing is one outflow. But there are several other ways in which resources are lost to the continent. Indeed, the reality of Africa is that the resources that leak out far exceed those that flow in. This is why Africa is a net exporter of capital.

And the sums are staggering. Previous estimates indicate that between 1970 and 2000 while Africa received about $100 billion in aid (including loans) it lost $274 billion in capital flight induced by debt, trade mis-invoicing and imputed interest. Add cumulative losses due to terms of trade for non-oil producing sub-Saharan African countries, estimated by the World Bank to be in the area of $400 billion or 120 per cent of combined GDP. Add also losses that African countries have incurred simply by opening up their markets.

African countries were made to reduce their rates of protection at a pace three times as fast as the countries of the Organisation for Economic Cooperation and Development (OECD). This has left the continent ridiculously open, relative to its stage of development. Christian Aid recently calculated that over the past two decades

---

*Africa is not as poor or as helpless as is often presented.*

*Instead, it is a continent that leaks heavily.*

*The task is to plug these leaks.*

---

Africa lost, in terms of income, the equivalent of over $270 billion just from the negative growth effects of trade liberalisation. This amount alone more than matches the accumulated value of grants, loans and net FDI channelled into the continent.

Add losses due to tax competition, tax evasion and tax avoidance. Taxation has served developed countries well as a means of redistribution and source of investment capital but it has been undermined through the enforced deregulation which has promoted tax competition, tax avoidance and tax havens. As a result, whereas government revenue from taxation in developed countries average 30 per cent of GDP between 1990 and 2000, in sub-Saharan Africa this has declined over the years to an average of 17.9 per cent of GDP.

Losses from tax competition have largely benefited multinational corporations whilst the tax burden has been transferred to wage earners and small businesses. Some analysts suggest that African oil producers command less than 20 per cent of the profits. The rest are lost to a complicated network of unfair trade practices. The transfer of revenues to tax havens by these corporations and rich individuals further exacerbates the revenue loss. It is estimated that at least $11.5 trillion is currently held in about 74 tax havens – lost to tax authorities – by wealthy individuals. This does not include laundered profits of businesses which operate through tax havens to avoid tax, nor does it include money illicitly transferred abroad through corruption, drugs and money laundering. These latter elements in any case comprise a much smaller share of resource losses than is generally believed.

As is obvious from above, Africa is not as poor or as helpless as is often presented. Instead, it is a continent that leaks heavily. The task is to plug these leaks. To do so, African civil society must turn attention to addressing:

- Support for campaigns aimed at corporate transparency
- Campaigns against tax concessions and for progressive tax policies

- Work with relevant networks to campaign for the end to banking secrecy and tax havens
- Follow-up on the recommendation of the Africa Commission report to pursue and return stolen wealth from Africa and to put in place measures to discourage illicit transfers abroad.

Incidentally, taxation and reliance on domestic sources for financing development also provide a more conducive environment for promoting democratic accountability than the dependence on aid. We have an obligation to plug the leaks.

# FOR LIFE OR PROFIT? GATS AND THE EXTERNALISATION OF AFRICA'S RESOURCES

### ODUOR ONGWEN

February 2006

The time is fast approaching when water, healthcare and every other essential service becomes tradable – with enormous implications for the lives of the poor and vulnerable. Oduor Ongwen, the country director of SEATINI Kenya, describes the international agreement that is going to regulate trade in services, the General Agreement on Trade in Services (GATS), noting that it is a 'dangerous instrument for the externalisation of resources of underdeveloped countries such as those in Africa'.

The service industry is quickly replacing trade in goods as the motor for global economic activity. From tourism to auditing services and from transport to insurance, the frontiers for economic domination are increasingly shifting from industry – manufactures and commodities – to trade in services. Services are currently the fastest growing component of trade and foreign direct investment (FDI), accounting for nearly 25 per cent of world trade and more than 76 per cent of FDI flows. It is for this reason that it was agreed at the launch of the Uruguay Round of trade negotiations in 1986 to include trade in services in the negotiations, in the belief that this would improve the world trade system.

But liberalisation of trade in services could be an uncontrolled avenue for indiscriminate investment deregulation and privatisation of vital public services, as well as giving foreign interests a foothold in government procurement. It could thus be a dangerous instrument for the externalisation of resources of underdeveloped countries such as those in Africa.

## Externalisation of Africa's resources

While those in control of the commanding heights of the global economy would like to convince us that globalisation is a new phenomenon made inevitable by the qualitative development of productive forces, we know better. Africa and the rest of the Third

World have been integrated into the global economic system since the mid-15th century. Unwillingly, Africa was part of the then dominant international trading system where its role was to supply natural resources in the form of gold, ivory, cloves, etc, and human resources in the form of slaves to the 'developed' world.

The second wave of globalisation followed the 1884 Berlin Conference, where the 'scramble for Africa' was concluded with the continent being divided amongst the leading colonial powers. Africa was then assigned the role of producing primary commodities – agricultural products, minerals, wildlife resources – for processing and manufacturing interests in the so-called 'mother countries'.

Almost half a century after the formal defeat of colonialism, the division of labour not only persists, but has also been revised and reinforced through corporate-led globalisation. We can identify 13 avenues for the externalisation of Africa's resources, which include, but are not limited to: debt servicing; difference in interest rates between North and South; unfair terms of trade; corporate control of world trade; capital account liberalisation; profit repatriation by transnational corporations; privatisation of state-owned enterprises; intellectual property rights; ecological debt; capital transfer; brain drain; immigration laws; and transfer pricing. Liberalisation of trade in services facilitates all these 13 avenues in haemorrhaging Africa's resources.

## Trade in services

Defined in broad terms, a service is a product of human endeavour aimed at satisfying a human need, but which cannot be categorised as a good. Others have simply defined a service as 'a product that cannot hit your foot'. However, the General Agreement on Trade in Services (GATS) does not define what constitutes a 'service'; instead, a guide to the GATS lists 12 major categories covering more than 160 distinct services. These services cover the gamut from birth to death.

The above understanding of services can be misleading since in reality services can be embodied in tangible products. For instance, a magazine is a good while an advertisement appearing in the magazine is a service. Publishing of the magazine is also a service.

GATS is the first and only set of international rules to open up trade in services to competition from foreign firms. Signed in 1994, it has nothing to do with whether the service is provided efficiently or not. It is a corporate boot sale of essential services ranging from water to electricity and the media.

The agreement, as pointed out earlier, covers 12 broad categories: communications; construction and engineering; distribution, wholesale and retail trade; education; energy; environment; financial services (including banking and insurance); health and social services; tourism and travel; sports, culture and entertainment; transport; and 'other', in case anything is not covered by the foregoing.

But critics warn that the reach of GATS could even extend to essential services such as education and health, resulting in their commercialisation by trans-national corporations. The naked truth is that, in the GATS lexicon, 'public service' is an aberration. Article I of GATS starts with a proclamation that the agreement does not apply to 'services provided in the exercise of governmental authority'. This would be great if it

---

*All human activities are to become, in the fullness of time, profit-oriented commodities that can be invested in, bought and sold.*

---

was not neutralised by the proviso that such governmental services must be supplied 'neither on a commercial basis nor in competition with one or more service suppliers'.

In the real world, perhaps it is only in Cuba or the Democratic Republic of Korea that there might be some public services that are not delivered on a commercial basis or in competition with other suppliers.

The logic and significance of GATS is easy to comprehend. All human activities are to become, in the fullness of time, profit-oriented commodities that can be invested in, bought and sold. And the agreement makes this irreversible since it is not a finished treaty but an open-ended framework agreement that mandates 'successive rounds of negotiations' with the goal of attaining 'progressively higher' levels of liberalisation.

This means that what is not opened today will be dealt with tomorrow until, presumably, all services are opened to all consumers by all countries in all 'modes' of delivery. Even more alarming is Article IV. It gives GATS powers to interfere, via the World Trade Organisation's (WTO) Dispute Settlement Body (DSB), with government efforts to pass 'measures' – laws, rules, regulations, procedures, administrative actions or any other forms – that are deemed to be 'unnecessary barriers to trade in services'. In other words, let not your pesky national standards stand in the way of foreign corporate interests.

As an example, one of the sectors that has been presented as being of great benefit to African countries is tourism. It has been posited that with full or substantial liberalisation of tourism, African beaches, nature parks and cultural attractions would be bursting at the seams with overseas visitors who would bring in an abundance of the 'scarce yet much needed' foreign exchange. These benefits are at best exaggerated and worst non-existent. 'Leakages' are encouraged thanks to the inordinate dominance of foreign ownership in the tourism industry. Leakage is described as a process through which part of the foreign exchange earnings generated by tourism, rather than being retained by tourist-receiving countries, is either retained by tourist-generating countries or remitted back to them. This foreign domination of the tourism sector in Africa has intensified under the GATS framework.

## The liberalisation of financial services: a casino economy

A typical Third World lesson in financial liberalisation could be distilled from the case of the Uganda Commercial Bank (UCB). Having yielded to the pressure from international financial institutions, the Uganda government sold off this national asset to Stanbic Bank. UCB had an extensive network all over the country, catering for rural farmers, teachers and civil servants. Most of the branches operated in UCB's own premises.

No sooner had the sale agreement been concluded than Stanbic closed down all the rural branches, sold the buildings (in the process realising more than four times what it had paid as purchase price) and repatriated the proceeds. No one cared that teachers who used to receive their salaries through the bank now had to spend two days every month and more money to reach the nearest bank. This is done at the expense of their pupils.

---

*A key concern is that through liberalisation schemes, water*
*is treated like any other commodity: to be sold at a profit.*
*Yet we know that water is essential to life and nature.*

---

A good number of WTO members have made commitments in financial services. These cover banking, insurance, securities and capital accounts. A smaller number have made commitments regarding insurance intermediation and the transfer of financial information. Fewer still have made a commitment with respect to derivatives trading. African countries and China have been cautious. The following could explain why.

On 2 July 1997 Thailand's currency, the baht, had to be floated. Far from being an isolated single country issue, this ignited the financial and currency crisis that was to engulf the East Asian sub-region. This crisis thrust millions of workers, small business enterprises, children and other vulnerable segments of the human race into dire poverty and desperation. The crisis quickly spread beyond the sub-region. Russia virtually succumbed to financial collapse; the Republic of South Africa had to intervene with a raise in interest rates so as to defend its currency. In quick succession, Brazil joined the ranks of crisis countries.

The crisis and its bushfire-like spread have forced certain issues into the domain of international discourse. The question arises as to what extent are the flaws inherent in the current dominant economic order responsible for the trend of slowing economic development and worsening global income distribution. This issue informs present debate over the global financial architecture.

The debate is carried from two poles. On the one hand is the Washington Consensus or Wall Street pole, which maintains that the crisis – and indeed global economic growth generally – is best addressed by more open trade, export led, greater deregulation and more liberalised financial markets. According to this school of thought, all that is required is a minor tune-up of the international financial system.

On other hand is the 'main-street alternative', which thinks the Washington Consensus model is irreparably flawed and fundamentally bankrupt. This viewpoint contends that the issue is not one of re-calibrating the model, but rather of designing a new model that is stable, equitable and pro-poor.

When it comes to financial architecture, the fundamental differences between the main-street alternative and the Washington Consensus become clear. The latter promotes and uses institutions it controls to impose opening up of the domestic financial markets, better accounting standards, more financial transparency and disclosure, and more International Monetary Fund surveillance.

For its part, the main-street alternative maintains that while improved accounting standards, financial transparency and disclosures are necessary, there is an acute need to reduce speculation and make long-term investment, giving proper regard to risk. This requires taxes on the buying and selling of currencies to reduce speculative trading, as well as requiring the investors to commit their investment to a minimum time period.

## Water for life or profit?

A key concern is that through liberalisation schemes, water is treated like any other commodity: to be sold at a profit. Yet we know that water is essential to life and nature. Indeed, water is our common heritage and a public trust. According to a report in *The East African* newspaper, the water provision in the port city of Dar es Salaam has not improved since it was privatised, yet the World Bank-funded British firm Biwater has increased the charges manifold.

Today the global water industry is dominated by fewer than ten companies – the leading two being French firms, Vivendi and Suez (with a water revenue of US$11.9 and $8.84 billion respectively in 2001). In 2001, Vivendi and Suez were ranked at positions 51 and 99 respectively on the Global Fortunes 500. The two French companies are facing stiff challenges from the German company, RWE, which recently purchased Thames Water of the UK and American Water Works of the US. RWE is ranked 53 in the Global Fortune 500 with a US$2.8 billion water revenue in 2001. Other key players in the privatisation of water services include Bouygues (France), Bechtel (US), Severn Trent, Anglian Water and Kelda (all UK).

Hiking of water prices is not the only concern. Most of the companies entrenched in the water sector have bad records. In 1999, the UK's drinking water inspectorate

---

### Cocoa trade and children

**February 2006**

IF YOU'RE A CHOCOLATE connoisseur then there's justice in the trade that brings you the sweetness that melts in your mouth. But if you're a child labourer on a cocoa farm in Côte d'Ivoire then justice is likely to be a very long way away.

In Côte d'Ivoire, the estimates are that as many as 15,000 children are forced to work in the farming of cocoa, the plant that supports the chocolate industry. According to a report entitled 'Chocolate and slavery: child labour in Côte d'Ivoire', many of the children recruited are young boys between the ages of 12 and 16. They work under inhumane conditions and suffer extreme abuse. Many are trafficked from neighbouring countries, especially Mali, and are sold to cocoa farmers upon their arrival in Côte d'Ivoire.

There are over 600,000 cocoa farms in the country, and one-third of the country's economy is based on the exports of this product. A substantial 43 per cent of cocoa beans used to feed the global market comes from Côte d'Ivoire, says 'Don't buy Nestlé until Nestlé buys fair trade!', a Global Exchange report. Numerous corporations benefit from the labour of those who work on these farms, but Nestlé SA is one of the most prominent. With annual sales of over $65 billion, it is one of the world's largest manufacturers of chocolate. It is also the third largest exporter of cocoa from regions in Africa, including Côte d'Ivoire, the report from the Global Exchange says.

**Sources**
'Chocolate and slavery: child labour in Côte d'Ivoire': http://www.american.edu/TED/chocolate-slave.htm
'Don't buy Nestlé until Nestlé buys fair trade!': http://www.globalexchange.org/getinvolved/actnow/nestleslavery.html

---

declared the Suez subsidiary, Northumbrian Water, the second worst company in terms of operational performance in England and Wales. The main reason was poor quality: high levels of iron and manganese were found in the water Northumbrian was delivering.

In the UK, five water companies – Anglian, Severn Trent, Northumbrian, Wessex and the Kelda Group – were successfully prosecuted 128 times between 1989 and 1997. On one count in August 2001, Thames Water pleaded guilty and was fined £26,600 for allowing raw sewage to pollute a stream within a few metres of a residential estate.

## Liberalisation and healthcare

Gradually but steadily there has been a major shift in global health strategy in recent years. Thanks to the Washington Consensus, the responsibility for healthcare provision has moved from the state to 'market forces'. The defining feature of this shift is many deaths from otherwise preventable and treatable diseases; the resurgence of diseases that humanity thought were already conquered like tuberculosis; and the detention of decomposing corpses in ghettoes, christened 'private clinics', for lack of payments.

David Werner, the author of the renowned and best-selling book *Where There Is No Doctor* is very clear on why the public should be worried about the shift in global and national health strategies. He recalls how the celebrated concept of universal primary healthcare had been adopted by virtually all governments at the landmark global health conference that endorsed the Alma Alta declaration.

To advance toward 'Health for all by the year 2000', the declaration promoted the principles that all people are entitled to basic health rights and that society (and thus the government) has a responsibility to ensure that the people's health needs are met, regardless of gender, race, class, relative ability or disability. The centrepiece of the declaration was primary healthcare, a comprehensive strategy that included an equitable, consumer-centred approach to health services and also addressed the underlying social factors that influence health.

## Hong Kong: the last nail

At the recently concluded WTO meeting in Hong Kong, developed countries bulldozed through a framework for GATS negotiations that compels countries to negotiate a minimum number of sectors with targets and indicators. These proposals will seriously erode the current flexibilities embodied in the GATS agreement. These flexibilities were the very reason for African countries' consent to GATS during the Uruguay Round. Furthermore, these proposals would completely change the very architecture of GATS and the approach to the negotiations as agreed in the negotiating guidelines.

Annex C introduces multilateral and sectoral approaches to the negotiations, which would force African and other developing countries to enter into negotiations in certain sectors, even if they are not yet ready to do so. Sectors that have been mentioned for sectoral negotiations include energy, water (through environmental services) and health (through financial services) – all of which are crucial and sensitive in African countries. Given Africa's level of development, selling out these sectors to market forces would pose serious threats to the affordability and accessibility of these services for the poor and vulnerable.

## Quick facts on trade

COLTAN, USED IN the manufacture of mobile phones (and exported mostly to the US), was sold by the Rwandan Army through Rwandan Metals at $200 per kg, at the rate of at least 100 tonnes a month in the late 1990s.
http://www.globalissues.org/Geopolitics/Africa/DRC.asp#AnInternationalBattleOverResources
http://us.oneworld.net/article/view/71424/1/

UGANDA'S TEXTILE SECTOR used to employ 500,000 people and earn $100 million in annual exports, but has virtually been brought to its knees by imports.
http://www.newint.org/issue373/currents.htm

FARMERS IN G8 COUNTRIES are subsidised approximately $1 billion a day, which is roughly equivalent to the entire GDP of sub-Saharan Africa.
http://www.washingtontimes.com/upi-breaking/20040725-031636-7601r.htm

FORCED TRADE LIBERALISATION has cost sub-Saharan Africa US$272 billion over the past 20 years.
The amount of money lost as a result of trade liberalisation could have paid all of these countries' debts and paid for the vaccinations and school fees of every child.
http://www.christian-aid.org.uk/indepth/506liberalisation/index.htm

 THE PRIVATISATION OF WATER in Ghana has meant that fees have increased by 95 per cent and will probably rise by another 300 per cent to meet the 'market rate'.
http://www.wsws.org/articles/2002/sep2002/wate-s07.shtml

 FOR EVERY DOLLAR in grant aid to developing countries, more than $13 go back to the North in debt repayments.
http://www.newint.org/issue365/facts.htm

 24 SUB-SAHARAN AFRICAN countries face food emergencies. Some 30.5 million people will need food assistance.
http://www.fao.org/newsroom/en/news/2005/107852/index.html

 IF TERMS OF TRADE for non-oil exporting countries in Africa had not declined over the past 20 years, the current level of per capita income would have been as much as 50 per cent higher after adjusting for inflation.
http://www.newint.org/issue374/facts.htm

IN THE LAST FOUR YEARS the US, Britain and France earned more income from arms exports to Africa, Asia, the Middle East and Latin America than they provided in aid.
http://www.newint.org/issue367/facts.htm

February 2006

# PRESERVING DISORDER – IMF POLICIES AND KENYA'S HEALTHCARE CRISIS

**SOREN AMBROSE**

June 2006

Compared to 20 years ago, people in Kenya live for ten years fewer on average, more children die in infancy and a greater proportion of those who survive face stunting. Why? Soren Ambrose makes a case for holding the International Monetary Fund (IMF) responsible, arguing that the institution's obsession with low inflation rates – one of the foundations of trade liberalisation – starves economies and hurts the poor.

On 6 March 2006 Kenya's assistant minister for health, Enock Kibunguchy, told the press that Kenya urgently needs to hire 10,000 additional professionals in the public health sector, blurting out: 'We have to put our foot down and employ. We can tell the International Monetary Fund and the World Bank to go to hell.'[1]

These are strong words for a high-ranking government official to put on record regarding the most powerful international financial institutions (IFIs), and in particular the IMF, a body whose power extends to being able to call for the withdrawal of virtually all external assistance to a country.

Minister of Health Charity Ngilu had in fact been rumoured to have made similar accusations in meetings with IMF officials and civil society representatives; since Kibunguchy's declaration she has confirmed she shares his view. Similar allegations have also been made by several civil society organisations, focused on the IMF and on health rights. Indeed, in the last two years a number of organisations have identified IMF restrictions as a serious disincentive to hiring desperately needed health professionals not only in Kenya but in many other African and global South countries as well.

Specific IMF policies, in particular the low ceilings it sets for inflation rates and wage expenditure in borrowing countries, are demonstrably illogical and detrimental. Together with the dubious defence the IMF mounts for maintaining such restrictions, cases like Kenya's provide a strong argument that those controlling the IMF should re-examine the restrictions it places on borrowing governments. The logic of demanding continual decreases in public wage bills is likewise suspect, as are the IMF's routine inflation targets. With increased funding from new sources, improved standards of living are within reach of even the most impoverished countries, if only the IMF would allow it.

## The healthcare crisis

Kenya's healthcare crisis has been 20 years in the making. Its dimensions are spelled out in the 2004 poverty reduction strategy paper (PRSP) – a government document written in consultation with the IMF and World Bank and approved by both bodies' boards. Life expectancy declined from 57 years in 1986 to 47 in 2000; infant mortality increased from 62 per thousand in 1993 to 78 per thousand in 2003; and under-five mortality rose from 96 per thousand births to 114 per thousand in the same period. The percentage of children with stunted growth increased from 29 per cent in 1993 to 31 per cent in 2003, and the percentage of Kenya's children who are fully vaccinated dropped from 79 per cent in 1993 to 52 per cent in 2003.[2]

Why this deterioration? As in most African countries, Kenya's healthcare system was hit hard by the 'structural adjustment' policies imposed by the IMF and World Bank as conditions on loans and as prerequisites for getting IFI approval of the country's economic policies. Those policies were introduced in the 1980s, and have left a lasting mark on Kenya's health. As usual with such programmes, the emphasis was on cutting budget expenditure. As a result, local health clinics and dispensaries had fewer supplies and medicines, and user fees became more common. The public hospitals saw their standard of care deteriorate, increasing pressure on the largest public facility, Kenyatta National Hospital in Nairobi. As a consequence, that hospital, once the leading health facility in East Africa, began, like so many other African hospitals, to ask patients' families to provide outside food, medicine and medical supplies. Most beds at Kenyatta and the regional and local hospitals accommodate two patients.

---

*As in most African countries, Kenya's healthcare system was hit hard by the 'structural adjustment' policies imposed by the IMF and World Bank as conditions on loans and as prerequisites for getting IFI approval of the country's economic policies. Those policies were introduced in the 1980s, and have left a lasting mark on Kenya's health.*

---

Professional staff have taken jobs – some part-time, some full-time – at private health-care facilities, or migrated to Europe or North America in search of better pay.

An October 2005 communication from an NGO coalition to the November 2005 High Level Forum on Health MDGs (Millennium Development Goals) notes that 'between 1991 and 2003, the [Kenyan] government reduced its work force by 30 per cent' – cuts that hit the health sector particularly hard.[3] For the period between 2000 and 2002 alone, the government was scheduled to lay off 5,300 health staff.

Those requirements were externally imposed. A World Bank Group document from November 2003, written to justify waiving a loan condition calling for a workforce reduction, notes: 'This condition required retrenching 32,000 personnel from civil service over a period of two years. In practice, 23,448 civil servants were retrenched in 2000/01 before the programme was interrupted by lawsuits. ... A specific commitment in the updated [agreement] is to reduce the size of the civil service by 5,000 per year through natural attrition.'[4] The very same document supports Assistant Minister Kibunguchy's assessment of the sector's current needs: 'the health sector currently experiences a staff shortage of about 10,000 health workers.' The document, however, draws no connection between the shortage and the insistence on cutting more workers.

The impact of the layoffs and budget slashing in the health sector over the last 15 years was cited recently by Member of Parliament Alfred Nderitu as the primary motivation for his motion of censure against the IMF and World Bank in the Kenyan parliament. His initiative would insist that any future loans from the institutions would need parliamentary approval.[5]

## Clinics without nurses

Many African countries have shortages of medical staff because of a lack of training capacity; in Kenya this is not the case. Thousands are unemployed or underemployed, eager to take up full time positions.

Both the Kenyan government and the IFIs regularly announce that health spending will increase substantially.[6, 7] With all these promises of increased resources for healthcare, with the World Bank's acknowledgement of a staff shortage, and with all those unemployed nurses, one might expect that the government would waste no time in hiring the thousands of nurses Kenya so desperately needs. And indeed, frequent promises are made by government officials to that effect. But the promises are almost never kept.

According to the chief economist in the Ministry of Health, S.N. Muchiri, the reason is that while the IFIs support increased expenditure on health, they forbid spending that money on staff wages. This is accomplished through insisting on a ceiling on wage expenditure; in Kenya, the targets are 8.5 per cent of GDP in 2006 and 7.2 per cent by

2008.[8] The IMF does not specify that hiring in the health sector must be limited, but when the entire wage bill must be suppressed, the chances of hiring the personnel needed are slim indeed.

So when IFI staffers call for more funding for clinics, as they do in their critique of the government's draft PRSP, they mean buildings, equipment, and medicine.[9] Unfortunately, personnel are required to run the clinics. It is the choice by those institutions to prioritise targets for reduced spending on public salaries and on inflation, says Muchiri, that prevents Kenya from hiring health workers.[10]

Muchiri provides valuable 'inside' confirmation of charges made with increasing intensity by civil society organisations over the last two years. Advocates point out that while recent funding initiatives like the Global Fund for AIDS, Tuberculosis and Malaria (GFTAM) and President Bush's Emergency Plan for AIDS Relief (PEPFAR) have made stemming the most critical health crises in Africa more possible, the IMF's power over borrowers' economic policy and its narrow focus on keeping inflation and payrolls as low as possible is actively discouraging governments from putting the available funds to use.

## Numbers, not people

On one level, it seems like commonsense for an organisation like the IMF to seek out ways in which governments can reduce the amount spent on salaries, especially in countries like Kenya, which have had trouble with 'ghost employees' on public payrolls in the past. But the self-defeating nature of this quest quickly becomes apparent. If the government were simply expected to identify and eliminate ghost employees, that would obviously lighten the government's burden and enable it to target its resources more wisely.

But the IMF's conditions deal with bottom-line expenditure, not with going to the root of the problem. Kenya's PRSP spells out the implications: '...achieving the 8.5 percent target by 2005/06 will require that any awards to be provided to the civil servants or any additional awards ... will be matched by a proportionate downsizing of the civil service.'[11] Any hiring of nurses, for example, would require that some other public employees be eliminated – regardless of how much the nurses may be needed, or how vital the other positions may be. Indiscriminate targeting like this only demonstrates the prioritising of abstract economic statistical standards over real-life outcomes, including those most likely to have a positive material impact on poverty and on contributing to the overall health of both Kenya's population and the economy.

So if the health budget is to rise – as both the IFIs and the government often repeat – then the PRSP must remind us that: 'The fiscal strategy assumes that these health expenditures will be focused on non-wage non-transfer expenditures and will thus enable the rapid increase in basic health services.'[12] Indeed, Muchiri reports that funds are often available for facilities or supplies, but not for staff. The result is that more people may seek out health services, but the ministry will actually be less able to provide them because of lack of personnel to administer the drugs or operate the machinery.

## Inflation, inflation, inflation

But why does the IMF, with its power to exclude a country from the global economy by declaring it 'off-track,' insist on reducing government payrolls? Adding employees to the government payroll, especially if accomplished with aid money, is considered by orthodox economists like those at the IMF to increase inflationary pressures in a developing country. And an increase in inflation is anathema to the IMF.

The IMF quite openly prioritises inflation targeting over almost any other factor in the countries where it works. Pressed on the question, as they have been in the debate over health spending, its officials will invariably respond that inflation is a 'tax' that hits the poor the hardest. But is that true? Anis Chowdhury points out that:

> The poor have very limited financial assets; they are largely net financial debtors. Thus inflation can benefit the poor by reducing the real value of their financial debt. Meanwhile, the IMF's cure for inflation – raising interest rates – can actually harm the poor because this increases the servicing costs of their current debts. … The poor fare worse when unemployment rises and persists, especially when there is no adequate safety net or social security system. At the same time, the real value of their household debt rises with falling inflation rates. Hence the poor have more reason to be averse to unemployment and less averse to inflation than the elite in society.[13]

After this seemingly obvious point is made, it seems only too easy to point out that those who stand to lose the most from inflation are those who hold large amounts of money – financiers, investors, bankers. Yes, there are risks to the poor in high and/or persistent inflation, but increases in inflation below a certain point are far more likely to cause pain to those whose incomes depend on relatively minor fluctuations in currency values. For the impoverished, as Chowdhury explains, such increases in inflation are likely to be more beneficial than harmful.

As is so often the case, it is easiest to discern the interests of policy-makers not from their rhetoric, but from whose interests are most vigorously protected by their policies – by who 'wins' as a result. The IMF's long-time prioritisation of inflation over all else lends weight to those who accuse it of using its powers to protect the interests of the wealthy over those of the impoverished, regardless of their rhetoric that maintains the reverse.

IMF official Andy Berg recently admitted as much: 'Higher inflation ... tax[es] people who hold cash or whose nominal incomes are fixed.' But Berg's next sentence restores IMF ideology, and at the same time exposes its flimsiness: 'And this tax discourages private investment and tends to fall on those least able to adapt – in other words the poor.'[14] Berg relocates the pain from the rich to the poor, but offers no logic for that move.

## Drawing a reasonable line on inflation

To challenge the IMF, the question must be where to draw the line – at what point, to use Berg's phrase, is 'inflation out of control', or at risk of spinning out of control? Berg says 'in poor countries the danger point is somewhere between 5 and 10 per cent'. The good news is that this figure is actually less conservative than the standard used in most IMF programmes. In most countries with IMF loans, the conditions call for inflation to decline and stay below 5 per cent.[15]

Few economists outside the IMF opt for a level as low even as 10 per cent in defining a healthy rate of inflation for a growing economy in a developing country. Terry McKinley, an economist with the United Nations Development Programme (UNDP), declares: 'As long as current revenue covers current expenditures, governments can usefully borrow to finance [social] investment. ... Fiscal deficits should remain sustainable as ensuing growth boosts revenue collection. The resultant growth of productive capacities will keep inflation moderate – namely, within a 15 per cent rate per year.'[16]

There is no room for neutrality in this debate. Adhering to IMF standards in order to avoid trouble will, according to McKinley, likely sabotage any hope of genuine development:

> Moderate inflation can, in fact, be compatible with growth. But low inflation can be as harmful as high inflation. When low-inflation policies keep the economy mired in stagnation or drive it into recession, the poor lose out, often for years thereafter, as their meager stocks of wealth are wiped out or their human capabilities seriously impaired. ... Without jobs and income, people cannot benefit from price stability.'[17]

Tactfully avoiding mentioning the IMF by name, McKinley argues:

> The new 'politically correct' justification for minimising inflation is that it hurts the poor. However, this misreads the facts: very high, destabilising inflation (above 40 per cent) definitely hurts the poor; and very low inflation (below 5 per cent) can also harm their interests when it impedes growth and employment.[18]

Rick Rowden points out that Latin American countries and 'East Asian tigers' like South Korea grew rapidly despite inflation rates of around 20 per cent.[19] But that was before the IMF moved into the development world in the 1980s, and re-wrote the rules – without any definitive evidence to support their claim that doing so was advantageous to the poor.

The IMF appears to be caught in a classic case of 'fighting the last battle'. When the IMF started lending to developing countries in the early 1980s, they were afflicted with astronomical, runaway inflation. It still apparently believes that hyperinflation is the most dangerous threat. But hyperinflation has been eliminated almost everywhere (apart from crisis or pariah countries like Zimbabwe); indeed, most developing countries now have inflation rates well below 10 per cent, and many below 5 per cent.[20] This is largely as a result of the IMF's hyper-vigilance over the last 25 years. The problem today is not hyperinflation, but IMF-induced stagnation.

More and more economists – outside the IMF – are taking a more complex view of growth and inflation. Rather than insisting that a country has a demonstrated 'absorptive capacity' before increasing the flow of revenues, they look at the likely impact of

---

*the IMF and World Bank could reasonably be charged with genocide. 'The only difference from what happened in Rwanda is they don't use* pangas *[machetes]. They use policies.'*

---

increased flows. In the case of increased spending on healthcare, not only is employment created (if wage ceilings are set aside), but the population's overall economic capacity improves. Private-sector activity, rather than being discouraged by public funds, is spurred by the increasing availability of resources.

Muchiri, in Kenya's health ministry, concurs with McKinley's positions on inflation targeting, and with the view that public spending, especially on healthcare, will encourage growth. He acknowledges that his government has committed to a low inflation target – its 'Letter of Intent' to the IMF states: 'The monetary programme for 2004/05 is designed to reduce underlying inflation to 3.5 per cent.'[21] And thus far Kenya seems to be meeting that goal.

But, says Muchiri: '3.5 per cent is too low for an economy that is supposed to grow by 5 per cent. A certain level of inflation is healthy – you can't grow otherwise.' This recognition moves Muchiri to criticise officials of a nearby country who have told him they must limit expenditure on healthcare – even refusing funds from the GFTAM – in order to prevent any risk of inflation rising. That line of thinking is clearly reflected in the recent statements by Kibunguchy and Ngilu.

33

But finance ministers who have committed to the IMF's inflation targets, and in many cases made those targets the centrepiece of their macroeconomic policy, are deeply reluctant to do anything that might raise that rate. Not only would doing so risk IMF disapproval and blacklisting, but it would also be seen as reversing a position they have publicly, and politically, committed to. Until this logjam is broken, a higher quality of life – even life itself – will continue to elude many thousands.

Muchiri counts as a significant victory the recent concession made by the IMF, after substantial negotiations, that Kenya could hire more health professionals if it could find donors willing to provide extra funds who themselves were comfortable with the impacts – economic and otherwise – that hiring additional health staff might have. It is this concession that recently allowed Kenya to announce that it will use funds from the Clinton Foundation, PEPFAR, and the GFATM to hire upwards of 2,000 new nurses and other health professionals.[22] Unlike with previous pledges, advertisements for the positions are now appearing in newspapers.

But the very existence of these policies, and the fact that he must invest so much in winning exceptions to them, cause Muchiri to reflect on his experiences of watching mothers and children die in hospitals for lack of surgeons or a lack of capacity to offer preventive care, and speculate that the IMF and World Bank could reasonably be charged with genocide. 'The only difference from what happened in Rwanda is they don't use pangas [machetes]. They use policies.'[23]

**Notes**

1 Elizabeth Mwai (2006) 'Ignore the World Bank on health, says minister', *The Standard* (Nairobi), 7 March.

2 International Monetary Fund (IMF) (2005) 'Kenya: poverty reduction strategy paper' *IMF Country Report* 05/11, p. 9 (subsequently cited as 'PRSP').

3 'A joint NGO statement to the High Level Forum on Health MDGs,' October 2005, p. 3.

4 International Development Association (World Bank Group) (2003) 'Kenya – economic and public sector reform credit – release of second tranche – waiver of two conditions and amendment of development credit agreement', 20 November, para. 33, p. 10.

5 (2006) 'Plans to censure WB, IMF,' *Kenya Times*, 14 March.

6 PRSP, p. 18.

7 PRSP, p. 21.

8 PRSP, p. 19.

9 International Monetary Fund (IMF) (2005) 'Kenya: joint staff assessment of the poverty reduction strategy paper', *Country Report* 05/10, para. 33, p. 10.

10 S.N. Muchiri, chief economist, Ministry of Health, Kenya, interview with author, 21 March 2006, Nairobi, Kenya. All of Muchiri's quotes come from this interview.

11 PRSP, p. 20.

12 PRSP, p. 21.

13 Anis Chowdhury, 'Poverty reduction and the "stabilisation trap" – the role of monetary policy',

University of Western Sydney, draft available from a.chowdhury@uws.edu.au. Cited in Rick Rowden (2005) 'Changing course: alternative approaches to achieve the Millennium Development Goals and fight HIV/AIDS,' ActionAid International USA, p. 30 <http://www.actionaidusa.org/pdf/Changing per cent20Course per cent20Report.pdf>.

14 Andy Berg (2006) 'An interview with Andy Berg on the macroeconomics of managing increased aid inflows,' *IMF Civil Society Newsletter*, February.

15 Rowden, p. 30.

16 Terry McKinley, 'MDG-based PRSPs need more ambitious economic policies,' *United Nations Development Programme – Policy Discussion Paper*, p. 4.

17 McKinley, pp. 14–15.

18 McKinley, p. 16.

19 Rowden, p. 31.

20 Rowden, p. 21.

21 Republic of Kenya, letter to Rodrigo de Rato, managing director of the IMF, 6 December 2004. Published by the IMF as 'Kenya-Letter of Intent, Memorandum of Economic and Financial Policies and Technical Memorandum of Understanding'.

22 See Lucas Barasa (2005) '2,210 jobs lined up for nurses', *Daily Nation* (Nairobi), 9 August, and Francis Openda (2005) 'State to hire 1,420 more health workers,' *The Standard* (Nairobi), 12 October <http://allafrica.com/stories/200510110915.html>.

23 To see a related commentary, by Soren Ambrose and Walden Bello, go to http://www.commondreams.org/views06/0524-22.htm.

## The fight for water in Ghana

### June 2006

World Water Day 2005 saw Biwater – one of the multinational firms bidding for the privatisation of Ghana's water sector – withdraw its bid, reported Ghana's Business News. Ghana's government has been fighting, with the support of the World Bank and International Monetary Fund, for several years to privatise the nation's water in attempts to gain access to external assistance and loans. Ghana currently faces inadequate water provision, blamed on years of poor management, lack of investment and poor technical capacity. The government argues that the only way to improve the situation is to inject fresh income into Ghana Water and that the only way to do this is to privatise. Critics and activist organisations, such as the National Coalition Against Privatisation of Water, have been active in opposing the initiatives. They argue that, contrary to government assurances that the scheme will make water cheaper and more accessible, the plan will in fact only undermine access to safe water for all Ghanaians.

While Biwater withdrew its application to partner with the government, numerous other multinational corporations are still seeking involvement in the project, and the government has gone ahead and secured a grant of $103 million from the World Bank, reports Irin News. According to the consumer advocacy organisation Public Citizen, the mere prospect of the privatisation of water has had the effect of doubling tariffs, in order to 'condition' the water market for international competition. World Bank conditions also stipulate that no subsidies will be given to low-income houses and that water must be sold at full market rates.

Public Citizen brings to light some of the startling statistics: in a country where over half the population earns less than $1 a day, and 40 per cent of people fall below the national poverty line, over 35 per cent of Ghanaian's lack access to safe water, and almost 70 per cent have no sanitation services. Water related illnesses are the cause of over 70 per cent of diseases in Ghana. Studies in the early 2000s showed poor households spent between 18 and 25 per cent of their income on water alone. In these conditions water vendors can charge up to 10 times more than the official water provider.

In the light of these statistics, IMF and World Bank policies of 'increased cost recovery' and 'automatic tariff adjustment mechanisms' are considered by activists to deny basic human rights. With civil society locked out of any of the decision-making processes, many are concerned that Ghana's need for financial resources has inhibited any alternative water options, and that the government's action goes further to undermine access to one of the world's most basic rights.

**Sources**

GhanaHomePage (2005) 'Water privatisation suffers setback – Biwater pulls out' <http://www.ghanaweb.com/GhanaHomePage/NewsArchive/artikel.php?ID=77784>

'Ghana National Coalition Against the Privatisation of Water – Statement' <http://www.isodec.org.gh/campaigns/water/>

'Ghana: privatisation brings new investment to water company' <http://www.irinnews.org/report.asp?ReportID=45054>

Hillary Lindsay (2004) 'Like water for profit: an interview with Rudolph Amenga-Etego', The Dominion website <http://dominionpaper.ca/environment/2004/05/27/like_water.html>

Public Citizen, 'Ghana action alert' <http://www.citizen.org/cmep/Water/cmep_Water/reports/ghana/>

# THE NEW SCRAMBLE FOR AFRICA'S RESOURCES

### HENNING MELBER

February 2007

Henning Melber presents a 'state of the continent' report and comments on the 'new African order' as designed by the global power structures of the World Economic Forum.

Almost 50,000 people from social movements all over the world gathered in Nairobi in January 2007 at the World Social Forum (WSF). Initiated in the Brazilian city of Porto Allegre a few years ago, the forum is organised as a counter meeting to the annual World Economic Forum (WEF) held at this time of year in the Swiss town of Davos. The WEF brings together those in command of the world's politics and economy and those 'celebrities' who like to be close to them. They represent a world in which Africa remains at the receiving end of global power structures and is increasingly, once again, the object of external interests. This article summarises and comments upon recent developments on the continent.

## Old wine in new bottles

It is anything but new that Africa's human and other natural resources are the object of more or less systematic looting from the outside world. Whoever still believes that 'globalisation' is a very recent phenomenon simply needs to look at an African view of the devastating impact of the slave trade to understand 'how Europe underdeveloped Africa' (as the title of a seminal book published by the late Walter Rodney during the early 1970s put it). As Karl Marx observed (though in rather insensitive language) in his *Critique of the Political Economy*, the hunt for black skins signalled the dawn of capitalism.

After the transatlantic slave trade, the forms of brutal exploitation meted out through colonialism and imperialism have at least been modified by formal decolonisation processes. However, the 'winds of change' created sovereign African states whose societies largely remain characterised by the structural legacy of an externally oriented dependency. The beneficiaries of the limited socioeconomic development that has taken place are still mainly those based outside of Africa and the – all

*It is anything but new that Africa's human and
other natural resources are the object of more or less systematic
looting from the outside world.*

too often parasitic – small local elites, who exploit their political control over national wealth for their own gains.

Local elites collaborate with those operating from the outside, offering them the most convenient (and unashamed) access in return for the small slice of the cake they are able to keep for themselves in such sell-out deals. Seen in this light, some (if not most) of the recent critical accounts of the aggressive expansion of Chinese interests into African countries and societies and their collaboration with local autocratic elites and despots has a hypocritical taste about it, or at least displays a touch of amnesia. After all, the Chinese penetration only highlights once more the ugly face of predatory capitalism, which for far too long has been abusing the dependency of most of the continent. One is therefore tempted to wonder if the concern expressed is more about Western interests than the welfare of the African people, given that the forms and effects of what we witness today is anything but new. While this critical observation does not exonerate the at times appallingly imperialist nature of the Chinese expansion into Africa, it does undermine the credibility of those critics who find no similar words for the other forms of imperialism that for far too long were (and continue to be) crucially responsible for contributing to the misery of many of Africa's people.

## Africa since the end of the bipolar world order

The collapse of the Soviet empire and the end of more than 40 years confrontation between East and West was by no means 'the end of history' (as suggested by Francis Fukuyama). It was the beginning of a new global order for hegemonic rule with far reaching consequences for African governments. Gone were the days where in the midst of a cold war there was space for limited opportunistic bargaining, which allowed for a bit of strategic positioning. Not that this was necessarily in the best interests of African people: all too often, this constellation encouraged and protected self-enrichment schemes for dictators and/or small local elites through forms of rent seeking or sinecure capitalism, as examples from A (such as Angola) to Z (such as Zaire) document. The bipolar world order was in no way a suitable breeding ground for development 'from below', but offered parasitic agents the opportunity to position themselves as satellites in return for their own gains within the East-West polarisation.

The consolidation of the USA's dominance during the 1990s and its impact on the global order resulted in several changes for the African continent. A regionally inter-linked 'appeasement' strategy (with the Russian retreat from Afghanistan and the Cuban withdrawal from Angola) secured in southern Africa the final decolonisation of Namibia (1990) and paved the way for an end to apartheid and democratic elections in South Africa (1994). During this period the economic paradigms represented by the international financial institutions (World Bank and IMF) became the defining power. The World Trade Organisation (WTO) emerged as the broker to regulate the comprehensively binding system for the global exchange of

---

*Gone were the days where in the midst of a cold war*
*there was space for limited opportunistic bargaining,*
*which allowed for a bit of strategic positioning.*

---

goods. These regulating processes had far-reaching implications not only for 'classical' trade relations but also for the club of G8 members, who define the rather one-sided rules of 'global governance'.

## Towards a new African order: NEPAD and AU

Significant dynamics within Africa at the beginning of this century complemented the global rearrangements. With democratically elected and legitimised new governments in South Africa and Nigeria, the two economic powerhouses on the continent south of the Sahara left behind their pariah status and resumed continental leadership roles. At the turn of the millennium Presidents Thabo Mbeki and Olusegun Obasanjo emerged (with active support from Senegal, Algeria and Egypt) as new figureheads, representing the collective interests of the South and in particular Africa to the industrialised Western countries. Originally tasked to negotiate debt cancellation arrangements they moved on to seek new forms of interaction through the WTO. Akin to junior partners in the global market, they became the architects of what finally became the New Partnership for Africa's Development (NEPAD).

After an incubation period and presumably intensive political negotiations behind closed doors, this blueprint was upgraded to the status of an official economic programme and institution of the African Union (AU). The AU emerged from the parallel transformation of the Organisation of African Unity (OAU). In the course of this change, significant corrections were made to previously established continental policies, such as the almost sacred principle of non-intervention in the internal affairs of member states.

With much confidence and trust and the substantive political support offered by the G8 after its 2001 summit in Genoa, the NEPAD architects were able to bring back home the reassuring message that the industrial West was on board and willing to support the initiative. This contributed to its acceptance both in Africa and by the United Nations system, which in a general assembly resolution officially recognised NEPAD as the economic programme for Africa. While this looks like a success story, the critical policy issues were to some degree either aborted or at best watered down. The good governance debate, while to some extent imposed by the Western-capitalist hegemony, was not, after all, just cosmetic rhetoric, but in some cases was indeed a meaningful change from past practices of not questioning autocratic rule by African despots and oligarchies.

The AU constitution was adopted at the same summit in Durban at which NEPAD was incorporated. It introduced the concept of collective responsibility,

*Both the AGOA and the EPA negotiations seem to reflect less a genuine desire for fairer trade than a wish to secure access to relevant markets in the interest of the USA and the EU.*

which had been absent from the OAU constitution, justifying joint intervention for specified reasons. There have been several results of this change, including interventions such as those in Darfur, the DRC, the Ivory Coast, Liberia and Togo, which in different ways (and with varying degrees of success) have all sought to contribute to conflict reduction or the enhanced legitimacy of political systems. In contrast, the African Peer Review Mechanism (APRM), conceptualised by NEPAD as a cornerstone for enhancing the notion of good governance, did not meet expectations. The disappointment over non-delivery was perhaps greatest when it came to the absence of any determined policy action by the NEPAD initiators over Zimbabwe (where the South African president preferred his so-called silent diplomacy to any meaningful political intervention). Nonetheless, the demand for democracy, human rights and respect for constitutional principles articulated by the NEPAD blueprint as a prerequisite for sustainable socioeconomic development might have been a contributing factor in the new phenomenon of an increasing number of African heads of state more or less voluntarily (and peacefully) vacating their offices. (This does not mean, however, that the rotten apples have been eliminated, as Museveni, and even – though less successfully – Obasanjo and some others have shown in their recent efforts to extend their stay beyond their stipulated period of office).

## Greater competition in a multipolar world

Systematic new efforts to access African markets and tap into local resources became visible with the adoption of the African Growth and Opportunity Act (AGOA) by the out-going Clinton administration. Through this initiative the USA openly underlined the importance of Africa to its external trade relations (Africa ranks higher than Eastern Europe in the US trade balance). A breakdown of the AGOA trade volume, however, also discloses that with the exception of a few smaller niches (e.g. the temporary opportunities created for a locally based – though not owned – African textile industry with preferential access to the US market) the trade volume mainly consists of exporting US-manufactured high tech goods and machinery and importing oil, strategic minerals and other natural resources for meeting the demands of US-based industries.

Soon after AGOA was enacted, the trade department of the EU Commission in Brussels initiated negotiations for a rearrangement of its relations with the African, Caribbean and Pacific (ACP) countries through so-called economic partnership agreements (EPAs). The declared aim was to enter a post-Cotonou agreement phase which would comply with the demands for WTO compatibility. The EPA negotiations have since then entered a critical stage, meeting with resistance from many of the ACP countries. They are afraid of losing out on trade preferences and feel that Brussels seeks to

---

*It was the markets and producers of the industrialised OECD countries which were the one-sided beneficiaries of state protection and distorting subsidies.*

---

impose a one-sided trade regime in its own interests, one that also denies the declared partners the right to autonomous negotiations by redrawing the map of regional configurations in Africa to comply with EU expectations.

Both initiatives, AGOA and the EPA negotiations, seem to reflect less a genuine desire for fairer trade than a wish to secure access to relevant markets in the interest of the USA and the EU. The competition for preferential trade agreements with South Africa (successfully negotiated by the EU during the late 1990s and currently facing an impasse with regard to the USA) also illustrate that the industrialised states do anything but share the same interest when it comes to securing their individual links with other countries.

The new offensive pursued by China, which expands aggressively into African markets and seeks access to the fossil energy resources and other minerals and metals

41

it urgently needs to fuel its own further rapid industrialisation process, adds to the rivalry and conflicting interests. In a matter of time, India, Brazil and Russia (as well as a number of other actors such as Malaysia and Mexico) are likely to add further pressure to the scramble for limited markets and resources. This latest stage in the struggle of competing forces on the continent has resulted in a plethora of recent analyses dealing mainly if not exclusively with the impact of Chinese practices. Interestingly enough, EU and US policies and practices almost fade from the picture. The current gloomy prophecies present a rather one-sided story, which downplays or ignores the damaging external effects that the existing socioeconomic imbalances and power structures have created and consolidated. The criticism of China appears to be more an indicator of the West's fear of a threat to its interests than a genuine concern for the African people.

## Greater dependency or more room to manoeuvre?

The global initiatives for liberalisation under the WTO regime pose the question of whether the markets and producers in so-called developing countries are able to meet the challenges of relatively free competition with the industrialised world or instead require continued protection. At a closer look, it becomes obvious that this question is wrongly posed. It was indeed the markets and producers of the industrialised OECD countries which were one-sided beneficiaries of state protection and distorting subsidies. Any claims of fairness in trade and market relations are an illusion and ideological humbug.

Those advocating a liberalisation of trade relations contribute to the misperception that such steps would be identical, or at least similar, to a deregulation of exchange relations with goods. As a matter of fact, the trend is quite the opposite. The so-called liberal global trade structures and networks have never before been so contractually defined. Numerous additional rules, such as hygiene and sanitary specifications, at times regulate access to markets even more than tariffs. They are open to abusive control and in cases of disagreement could be used as a tool for sanctions.

However, historically structurally disadvantaged societies should at least be allowed to make socioeconomic gains as a result of their own initiatives. This requires a framework which would as a matter of principle allow some sort of protectionist policy to be a legitimate survival strategy to empower local producers and foster home markets. This could create conditions from which in subsequent exchange relations the people in both industrial and African societies could benefit (but perhaps at the expense of unhindered profit maximisation for those who earn most).

With new rivals such as China, India, Brazil, Russia and a series of other countries on the threshold of meaningful industrial production, the competition to enter favourable relations with African countries might increase. This is in itself not a threat to

## Export processing zones in Kenya

### February 2006

Export Processing Zones (EPZs) are areas where the normal rules governing trade simply do not apply. They exist solely to provide Western countries with cheap goods, produced with cheap resources and by cheap labour.

In Kenya, EPZs run a brisk business, with over 75 per cent of the produced goods being exported to America. The financial profits are huge, but reach only a limited few. Those who provide the labour see none of these profits and suffer human rights abuses.

Export processing zones enjoy tax breaks and are not subject to local regulations, including labour laws. They can thus earn millions of dollars, which they pocket entirely. In 2002 earnings in Kenyan EPZs were recorded at Ksh17.5 billion. In 2003 the exports valued Ksh13,273 million while the total domestic expenditure was Ksh5,085 million.

Kenya and Kenyans, however, see little of this money. According to a Global Policy report entitled 'Investor dollars versus workers' rights', the foreign companies that operate in the country are free to repatriate their profits. Labourers – who work under unhealthy and often dangerous conditions – earn as little as $1 a day. Manufacturers argue that wages are so low because they must import raw materials, pay expensive electricity costs and freight charges and have to deal with an unreliable infrastructure.

**Sources**
Review of 'Manufacturing poverty':  http://www.pambazuka.org/index.php?id=22712
'Investor dollars versus workers' rights': http://www.globalpolicy.org/socecon/inequal/labor/2003/0221investor.htm

the interests of African people, but it requires that the tiny elites who currently benefit from the existing unequal structures put their own interests in self-enrichment schemes behind the public interest to create investment and exchange patterns that first provide benefits for the majority of the people.

**Selected further reading**

Alden, C., Large, D. and Soares de Oliveira, R. (eds) (2007), *China Returns to Africa: The Politics of Contemporary Relations*. London: Hurst

Broadman, Harry G. et. al. (2007), *Africa's Silk Road. China and India's New Economic Frontier*. Washington: World Bank

Brüntrup, M., Melber, H. and Taylor, I. (2006) 'Africa, regional cooperation and the world market', *The Nordic Africa Institute Discussion Paper*, 31 (available from http//: www.nai.uu.se)

China in Africa issue (2006) South African Journal of International Affairs, 13 (1)

Fombad, Charles Manga and Kebonang, Zein (2006) 'AU, NEPAD and the APRM. Democratisation efforts explored', *Current African Issues*, 32 (available from http//: www.nai.uu.se)

Manji, Firoze and Marks, Stephen (eds) (2007) *African Perspectives on China in Africa*. Nairobi and Oxford:

Fahamu

Melber, Henning (2002) 'The New Partnership for Africa's Development (NEPAD) – Old wine in new bottles?', *Forum for Development Studies*, 29(1)

Melber, Henning (2004) 'The G8 and NePAD – more than an elite pact?', *University of Leipzig Papers on African Politics and Economics* (ULPA), 74

Melber, Henning (ed) (2005) 'Trade, development, cooperation. What future for Africa?' *Current African Issues*, 29 (available from http//: www.nai.uu.se)

Melber, Henning (ed) (2007) *China in Africa*. Uppsala: The Nordic Africa Institute (forthcoming)

Southall, Roger and Melber, Henning (eds) (2006) *The Legacies of Power. Leadership Transition and the Role of Former Presidents in African Politics*. Cape Town and Uppsala: HSRC Press and Nordic Africa Institute

Taylor, Ian (2005) *NEPAD. Towards Africa's Development or Another False Start?* Boulder and London: Lynne Rienner

Taylor, Ian (2006) *China and Africa. Engagement and Compromise*. London and New York: Routledge

Tull, Denis M. (2006) 'China's engagement in Africa: scope, significance and consequences', *Journal of Modern African Studies*, 44(3), pp. 459–79

# CHINA IN AFRICA

## STEPHEN MARKS

January 2007

Stephen Marks reviews the billion-dollar glamour on display in Beijing during a summit between African and Chinese leaders in early November 2006. But behind the glitz, what does it all mean for Africa? Is it colonialism revisited, a mad dash for African oil and minerals? Is there a Chinese model of development that can be followed? And what is the true nature of Chinese involvement in Africa?

Heads of state and dignitaries from 48 countries flocked to Beijing in November 2006 to attend the largest international summit ever held in the Chinese capital. And China pulled out all the stops, not only, or not even, to make the VIP guests feel welcome, but also to leave China's people and the world at large in no doubt of the meeting's importance.

Bright red banners lined the streets with slogans lauding 'Friendship, Peace, Cooperation and Development.' China's official news agency, Xinhua, declared that

> *Perhaps the material distinction is not*
> *between Chinese capital and Western,*
> *but rather between the merely rapacious,*
> *and the more sophisticated.*

the visitors 'brought a trend of the mysterious continent to the capital of China'.[1] Giraffes and elephants frolicking on the savannahs were spread over giant billboards on all the capital's main streets and squares.

'The CDs and DVDs on Africa are very popular, and some of the African musical products have been sold out,' Xinhua reported a shop assistant as saying. And 'In a restaurant of African food in the Chaoyang District, east of Beijing, it's hard to find a seat in the recent week. The unique foods and hot African dances attracted many people.'

But behind the official 'Africa chic' and the predictable warm words of the official communiqués, something substantial was going on. The declaration adopted at the end of the meeting on Sunday 5 November was strong on 'motherhood and apple pie' rhetoric, promising 'a new type of strategic partnership' founded on 'political equality and mutual trust, economic win-win cooperation and cultural exchanges'. But there was impressive substance too.

On Saturday 4 November, China's Premier Wen Jiabao proposed that China and Africa should seek to bring their trade volume to US$100 billion by 2010. This would more than double the 2005 level, about US$39.7 billion. In the first nine months of 2006, China–Africa trade had already surged to US$40.6 billion, up 42 per cent year-on-year.

On the same day China's President Hu Jintao announced a package of aid and assistance measures to Africa including US$3 billion of preferential loans over three years and the cancellation of more debt owed by poor African countries. China, he pledged, would:

- Double its 2006 assistance to Africa by 2009
- Provide US$3 billion of preferential loans and US$2 billion of preferential buyer's credits to Africa in the next three years
- Set up a China–Africa development fund, which would reach US$5 billion, to encourage Chinese companies to invest in Africa and provide support to them
- Cancel debt in the form of all the interest-free government loans that matured at the end of 2005 owed by the heavily indebted poor countries and the least developed countries in Africa that have diplomatic relations with China
- Increase from 190 to over 440 the number of export items to China receiving zero-tariff treatment from the least developed countries in Africa with diplomatic ties with China.
- Establish three to five trade and economic cooperation zones in Africa in the next three years
- Over the next three years, train 15,000 African professionals; send 100 senior agricultural experts to Africa; set up 10 special agricultural technology demonstration centres in Africa; build 30 hospitals in Africa and provide a grant of RMB 300 million for providing artemisinin[2] and building 30 malaria prevention and treatment centres to fight malaria in Africa; dispatch 300 youth volunteers to Africa; build 100 rural schools in Africa; and increase the number of Chinese government scholarships to African students from the current 2,000 per year to 4,000 per year by 2009.

President Hu even pledged to build a conference centre for the African Union 'to support African countries in their efforts to strengthen themselves through unity and support the process of African integration' – perhaps a visible reinforcement of the final statement's pledge to support 'the African regional and sub-regional organisations in their efforts to promote economic integration, and [support] the African countries in implementing the "New Partnership for Africa's Development" programs'.

Early on Sunday morning, the 2nd Conference of Chinese and African Entrepreneurs concluded with 14 agreements signed between 11 Chinese enterprises and African governments and firms, worth a total of US$1.9 billion. The agreements covered cooperation in infrastructure facilities, communications, technology and equipment, energy and resources development, finance and insurance.

The biggest deal was one worth US$938 million, for China's state-owned Citic conglomerate, to set up an aluminium plant in Egypt. There was also a new copper project, worth US$200 million, in Zambia, along with plans to build a US$55 million cement factory in Cape Verde. A mining contract with South Africa, worth US$230 million, was also announced.

There was more good news to come. The summit was followed by a two-day African Trade Fair in Beijing. According to Xinhua 'Over 170 enterprises from 23 African countries filled a Beijing exhibition hall on Monday with varieties of their local specialties, including minerals, jewelry, textile, fur, spice, tea and coffee.'

Zhao Jinping, deputy director of the foreign economy department under the State Council Development and Research Centre, told Xinhua that the summit's decisions 'offers Chinese private firms unprecedented opportunities to invest in Africa'.

But except for textiles, which are notoriously hard-hit by Chinese exports, all the items listed as on display were primary products which Africa was already exporting in colonial times. Perhaps this influenced Xinhua's choice of Chinese entrepreneurs to interview on their view of future business prospects in Africa:

Wang Jianping, president of the Hashan Company in eastern Zhejiang Province, told Xinhua that after the summit, he decided to increase investment in Nigeria from two million dollars to six million dollars so as to boost the development of local shoe-making industry.

Sheng Jushan, general manager of the Guoji Group in central China's Henan Province, said his company has just set up an economic cooperation zone in Sierra Leone, which attracts about 20 Chinese small and medium-sized enterprises.

A similar processing zone in Nigeria, according to Xinhua, 'when completed and put into operation, will help boost economic activities in the state through processing local raw materials into manufactured goods, especially those that have to be imported now in the country'.

## Colonialism revisited?

China's race for Africa is certainly due in large part to the same causes as Europe's 19th century scramble – the need for raw materials to fuel industrialisation. As *The Economist* summarised it before the summit:

> Its economy has grown by an average of 9% a year over the past ten years, and foreign trade has increased fivefold. It needs stuff of all sorts—minerals, farm products, timber and oil, oil, oil. China alone was responsible for 40% of the global increase in oil demand between 2000 and 2004.
>
> The resulting commodity prices have been good for most of Africa. Higher prices combined with higher production have helped local economies. Sub-Saharan Africa's real GDP increased by an average of 4.4% in 2001–04, compared with 2.6% in the previous three years. Africa's economy grew by 5.5% in 2005 and is expected to do even better this year and next.[3]

In Beijing in 2005 Moeletsi Mbeki, deputy chairman of the South African Institute of International Affairs, spelled out to a conference organised by the Chinese Parliament what many feared might be the result:

> Africa sells raw materials to China and China sells manufactured products to Africa. This is a dangerous equation that reproduces Africa's old relationship with colonial powers. The equation is not sustainable for a number of reasons. First, Africa needs to preserve its natural resources to use in the future for its own industrialisation. Secondly, China's export strategy is contributing to the de-industrialisation of some middle-income countries ... it is in the interests of both Africa and China to find solutions to these strategies.[4]

Clearly, many of the decisions announced at the summit reflect Chinese awareness of these fears of a 'new imperialism'.[5] So did the *People's Daily* article before the summit indignantly denouncing 'The fallacy that China is exercising "neo-colonialism" in Africa', which was 'apparently aimed at sowing discord between China and Africa'.[6]

And on the eve of the summit the state council, China's cabinet, issued 'Nine Principles' to 'Encourage and Standardise Enterprises' Overseas Investment'. The principles require Chinese companies operating overseas to 'abide by local laws, bid contracts on the basis of transparency and equality, protect the labor rights of local employees, protect the environment, implement corporate responsibilities and so on'.[7]

## Reviewing the issues

Clearly, to respond to the challenge of China's turn to Africa, activists will need to situate its actions against the background of its original source in China's raw material needs.[8] They will also need to keep abreast of the detailed impact of China's operations on the ground, including those cases where the rape of natural resources and the impact of infrastructure developments on land rights and on the environment is at its most destructive, and is most reminiscent of traditional colonialism.[9]

China's close links with Robert Mugabe, which he at least boosts as a model of the concept of 'win–win economic cooperation' deserves special attention[10] and the nature of China's development aid also needs analysis and comparison with others.[11]

> *one aspect of the 'Chinese model' which is certainly*
> *appealing to Africa's more repressive regimes is the idea*
> *that it represents a refutation of the view that democracy is*
> *an essential precondition for development*

Work in all these areas will need to continue; and Daniel Large's[12] critique of the idea of 'Chinese exceptionalism' should provide it with a sound foundation. But, as Michelle Chan-Fishel[13] points out, Chinese companies in their operations in Africa and at home appear to repeat the same environmentally and socially destructive model already exemplified by the West. A host of further question marks will therefore be raised over the widespread concept that China's own development path has lessons for Africa – an 'alternative Chinese way'.

## Is there a Chinese model?

The most obvious answer to the question is 'yes' in the sense that, like Japan and the smaller 'Asian tigers', China did not develop by following the rules of the Washington consensus. Critical attention in the West and also in Africa, has been focused on China's avoidance of the good governance and human rights conditionality now commonly insisted on by the West, and this undoubtedly lies behind much of the enthusiasm for the 'Chinese model' on the part of Africa's more repressive regimes.

But there is also substance to the idea that 'South–South' cooperation has merit in its own right. In areas such as rural development and intermediate technology China's experience does indeed have much to offer that is of greater relevance precisely because China too is a developing country.

As John Rocha points out,[14] codes such as the African Peer Review Mechanism were not intended to be part of an aid conditionality package, and the perception that they are externally imposed has damaged their reputation even in the eyes of campaigners and activists who support their objectives.

Conversely, China's avoidance of conditionality means that she can move faster to produce visible results on the ground. The statism which still characterises China's economy means that China can offer a 'one-stop shop' approach, in which contracts guaranteeing China its desired access to oil or key minerals, as in Angola or Nigeria, can be combined with soft loans and much-needed infrastructure projects such as highways and railways, and low-cost, high-impact 'add-ons' such as rural development projects, industrial parks for small firms, and training and scholarships.

Thus the BBC reported on 28 April 2006:

> Chinese President Hu Jintao has signed an important oil exploration agreement with Kenya during his trip to Nairobi. Six other deals have also been signed on malaria, rice and roads. Mr Hu is also due to visit wildlife parks that are eager to attract Chinese tourists. Kenya is keen to secure Chinese investment deals in the pharmaceutical and technology sectors.
>
> The president's trip has focussed on deals to expand Chinese investment in Africa's natural resources, especially oil, to satisfy China's energy-hungry economy.
>
> On Wednesday, China secured four oil-drilling licences from Nigeria in a deal involving $4bn in investment.
>
> The deals cover:
> - road maintenance in Nairobi
> - support for rice-growing schemes
> - maintenance of a sports centre
> - setting up an anti-malaria health centre.[15]

This integrated approach can be a genuine plus-point, and not only for such regimes as those in Zimbabwe or Sudan. As in this example, the whole deal can be tied up and delivered in visits by top governmental figures, reciprocated by red-carpet treatment for African leaders, as at the recent Beijing summit.

But not all these factors are unique to China, and future analysis would benefit by looking at China's approach in a wider context, rather than in the one-track contrast with the conventional model of liberal globalisation which characterises conventional Western approaches.

As Chris Melvile and Molly Owen have pointed out[16] China is not the only player in the 'South–South' game, or the only one to promote the idea as offering 'win-win' benefits. India, Brazil and South Africa have established their own 'south-south' links. Each has also been welcomed as an alternative to the old imperialist powers. And each in its turn has been accused of pursuing its own 'sub-imperialist' agenda.

And as Chris Alden and Martyn Davies point out:

> Chinese MNCs [multinational corporations] are in many respects like other MNCs operating in Africa, for example France's Elf-Aquitaine or South Africa's Eskom. In the French case, Elf-Aquitaine has been highly politicised, building up or even defining France's Africa policy in particular countries such as Gabon or Angola.
>
> The close proximity between French business and political interests manifested by the presence of oil company executives in the inner circle at the Elysee Palace as well as the circulation of key political elites such as Jean-Christophe Mitterrand within political and business circles, has been a feature of France's post-independence African policy from the outset
>
> Moreover the modus operandi of foreign policy makers in Paris has been to construct policy around a network of personal relationships with individual African leaders, bolstered by a web of bilateral agreements in trade, finance, development assistance and defence.[17]

## The nature of the Chinese multinational corporations

If the role of the Chinese state is not so different to that of at least some Western and 'Southern' states, how does the Chinese MNC itself differ from its rivals in the way in which it operates as a firm?

China's government made its position clear in its official policy statement on Africa: 'The Chinese Government encourages and supports Chinese enterprises' investment and business in Africa, and will continue to provide preferential loans and buyer credits to this end.'[18]

As Mark Sorbara puts it 'Investing in African extractive industries is a risky business, but China is desperately in need of raw materials to feed its booming economy, hence the government is willing to shoulder most of the risk for Chinese companies looking to invest in Africa'.[19]

But the purpose of this state backing is not only to secure China's access to raw materials. As Alden and Davies point out:

> In pursuit of its broader global ambitions, Beijing is intent on 'picking corporate champions' that, with the benefit of active and generous support from the state, are being groomed to join the ranks of the Fortune 500. Roughly 180 companies have been designated by the state to benefit from preferential finance, tax conces-

sions and political backing to 'go global' and become true multinationals.[20]

This aim to be global players in their own right was made clear by Fu Chengyu, chief executive of China's oil giant CNOOC after the US Congress moved to block CNOOC's takeover bid for Unocal, the US' ninth-largest oil firm: 'We aim to be a participant in the global industry, like all the international majors, supplying the global marketplace as well'.[21]

The same seems to apply to the China–South Africa deal, concluded at the Beijing summit, to set up a joint company to expand ferro-chrome production in South Africa. Reuters' report on the deal commented that 'China has become a big investor in mining and natural resources in Africa as it seeks the raw materials to feed its economic growth, but unlike many Sino-African deals the purpose of Tubatse Chrome is to make money rather than to supply metal to China'. And the chairman of the South African partner was quoted as saying: 'Sinosteel is a trading organisation, and Tubatse Chrome will be a profit-driven company. If China offers the best price we will sell it to China, but we will sell to wherever we can get the best price.'[22]

Optimists may view this as a good sign. As Ndubisi Obiorah puts it:

As Chinese companies move up the global pecking order and discover the considerable mark-up to be derived from possessing premium brands and intellectual property, they will seek to establish their own brands. As global branding and reputation become more important to Chinese companies, they may become less willing to be associated with human rights abuses and repressive regimes in Africa and elsewhere.[23]

As a result, he suggests, Chinese companies could become more vulnerable to 'naming and shaming' from NGO's in Western countries and elswhere.

Optimists may also see some signs of this on the websites of Sinopec and Petrochina, which feature prominently their awards for corporate governance, and their 'model' policies on health, safety and environmental protection.

Does this establish the need for a 'corporate China watch' to be set up, for activists in Africa and elsewhere to bring this pressure to bear? But in that case why single out China? As Alden and Davies conclude: 'Indeed even critics admit that if one sets aside the particular cases of Sudan, Angola and Equatorial Guinea, "the rest of PetroChina and Sinopec activities on the African continent are not especially reprehensible" or at least no more so than many of their Western counterparts.'[24]

Perhaps the material distinction is not between Chinese capital and Western, but rather between the merely rapacious, and the more sophisticated. Even these are not two separate categories, but at least as much two different faces, each of which may be presented as convenient.

In this context, those involved in corporate research could usefully examine the possibility that Chinese MNCs operating in Africa might themselves incorporate some Western capital, perhaps percolating not only through the obvious channel of joint ventures and shareholdings, but also through funds from Hong Kong and Taiwan.

Neil Tottman, head of commercial banking at HSBC China, has laid out aggressive plans for its commercial banking businesses in China, in anticipation of further deregulation of the sector this year. 'The total volume of business referrals between Hong Kong and the mainland grew at an annual rate of 175 percent between 2002 and 2005. This year to date, volume between Taiwan and the mainland has increased 512 percent over the same period last year.'[25]

## The antidemocratic road?

But there is one other aspect of the concept of a distinctive 'Chinese model' which is certainly appealing to Africa's more repressive regimes – the idea that it represents a refutation of the view that democracy is an essential precondition for development. The view is widely held that China proves the opposite – the need for strong government.

*It could also be pointed out that before 1949 some of the main obstacles to China's development were to be found in chronic national disunity and warlordism on a scale whose closest parallel in today's Africa is the Democratic Republic of Congo.*

Ndubisi Obiorah quotes a Nigerian example of this invocation of a 'Chinese model': 'leading lights of the Obasanjo faction claimed that an absence of stability and visionary leadership were the principal cause of Africa's underdevelopment and that it was these same qualities that had enabled Singapore and China to become contemporary economic miracles'.[26]

As Obiorah points out, the rise of India might counter this self-interested vogue for authoritarian government. It could also be pointed out that before 1949 some of the main obstacles to China's development were to be found in the close ties of ruling elites to forces at home and abroad opposed to modernisation; in archaic patterns of land ownership and authority; and in chronic national disunity and warlordism on a scale whose closest parallel in today's Africa is the Democratic Republic of Congo (DRC). All of these were swept away by a massive popular revolution – a prospect likely to be at least as unacceptable to Africa's current repressive elites as a more gradual and

## Soweto fights for electricity

June 2006

Eskom, the country's electricity provider, has featured predominantly in recent South African news because of continuing power outages in various parts of the country. But these power outages have not affected many in the townships that house the majority of the nation's black population. Soweto, in Johannesburg, is the largest of these townships, and is home to several million working-class people, most of whom struggle to make ends meet. Electricity is simply too expensive for many, and as a result, they make do with alternative forms of lighting, heating and cooking.

In 1996 the African National Congress (ANC) adopted neoliberal policies, turning their back on a proposed reconstruction and development programme (RDP), and opting instead for the GEAR programme. The GEAR programme was developed by economists and World Bank officials and, as a neoliberal programme, emphasised growth, adding that redistribution would come only after growth. Meant to drive this growth, targets were set to reduce inflation, boost the private sector and liberalise formerly government-run agencies, including Eskom. In order to attract investors and offer a return on investment, Eskom set about increasing profits through a strict system of cost recovery.

In places like Soweto this meant that electricity cut-offs were made as a means of recouping debt and making sure people paid for their electricity use. According to activist Trevor Ngwane, at one point Eskom was cutting off over 20,000 homes a month and over 70 per cent of Soweto's population had increasing debts to the company. The Soweto Electricity Crisis Committee, co-founded by Ngwane, was formed to unite Soweto against electricity cut-offs. It claimed as its slogan: 'Electricity is a right, not a privilege.' The group lobbies government and other policy groups and, significantly, reconnects those homes that have been cut off, providing residents with the electricity they need. Their work has spread beyond Soweto, and they are active all over South Africa, campaigning now not only for electricity, but also water. Their approach is one of participatory democracy: they call for policies that respond to the needs of the people – that is, the poor, who make up the majority of South Africa – and demand free services, including electricity, water, housing, healthcare and education, for all. The Soweto Electricity Crisis Committee sees itself as a part of a larger anti-globalisation, anti-capitalist movement, and calls for people around the movement to join hands to fight against imperialism and anti-poor policies.

**Source**

Article based on an interview between Trevor Ngwane and Walter Turner on KPFA's 'Africa Today' <http://www.warprofiteers.com/article.php?id=11501>.

reformist path to democratisation!

But the most powerful antidote to the idea that China validates an authoritarian road to development is the growing grassroots unrest in China over the cost of the country's current economic model in its impact on employment rights, the environment and mounting inequality and social exclusion.

As Dorothy Guerrero has pointed out:

> China is now the world's fourth-largest economy and many developing countries envy its record of economic progress. However, China's phenomenal growth is producing a big misconception in that it is viewed as a big winner of globalisation.
>
> Although it is true that market reforms and China's opening to the global economy gave millions of people there an increased standard of living, more Chinese people are suffering the consequences of its rapid transition to a market-based economy.
>
> The majority of the Chinese people are not too concerned about when China will become the world's largest economy. Rather, they are asking, 'When will the benefits of China's rise to superpower status start to affect our lives positively?'[27]

Even official sources in China and abroad are aware of the social costs of China's free-market great leap forward. Members of the legislature have warned of the country's impending employment crisis[28] and the World Bank has confirmed that China's poor are getting poorer.[29]

As for the environment, no less a figure than Pan Yue, deputy director of China's State Environmental Protection Administration, sparked controversy with a recent essay *On Socialist Ecological Civilisation* when he openly charged that: 'The economic and environmental inequalities caused by a flawed understanding of growth and political achievement, held by some officials, have gone against the basic aims of socialism and abandoned the achievements of Chinese socialism.'[30]

The march of neoliberalism within China and its impact on the Chinese people has advanced hand-in-hand with China's growing imperialist role abroad.[31] This apparent anomaly of an imperialist power itself subject to growing imperialist exploitation in alliance with local capital is not new – it also characterised Czarist Russia. And difficult though it may currently seem to act on the idea, the connection suggests that an obvious grassroots ally of activist and civil society groups in Africa will increasingly be their opposite numbers in China itself.[32]

### Notes

1 For all references to official documents and speeches at the November summit, and to Xinhua coverage of it, see the official summit website at http://english.focacsummit.org/.

2 A drug extracted from a shrub and used to treat malaria in Chinese traditional medicine.

3 *The Economist* (2006) 'Never too late to scramble', 26 Oct <http://www.economist.com/world/africa/

displaystory.cfm?story_id=8089719>.

4 M. Mbeki (2006) *South African Journal of International Affairs*, 13(1):7.

5 Stephen Marks (2006) 'China in Africa – the new imperialism?', *Pambazuka News*, 244, 2 March <http://www.pambazuka.org/en/category/features/32432>.

6 People's Daily Online (2006) 20 October <http://english.people.com.cn/200610/30/eng20061030_316577.html>

7 Scott Zhou (2006) 'China as Africa's angel in white', *Asia Times*, 3 November <http://www.atimes.com/atimes/China_Business/HK03Cb04.html>.

8 See John Rocha (2007) 'A new frontier in the exploitation of Africa's natural resources: the emergence of China', in Patrick Burnett and Firoze Manji (eds) *African Perspectives on China in Africa*. Nairobi and Oxford: Fahamu.

9 See Anabela Lemos and Daniel Ribeiro (2007) 'Taking ownership or just changing owners?', reporting on Mozambique, and Ali Askouri (2007) 'China's investment in Sudan: displacing villages and destroying communities', both in Patrick Burnett and Firoze Manji (eds) *African Perspectives on China in Africa*. Nairobi and Oxford: Fahamu.

10 See John Karumbidza (2007) 'Win-win economic cooperation: can China save Zimbabwe's economy?', in Patrick Burnett and Firoze Manji (eds) *African Perspectives on China in Africa*. Nairobi and Oxford: Fahamu.

11 See Moreblessings Chidaushe (2007) 'China's grand re-entrance into Africa – mirage or oasis?', Patrick Burnett and Firoze Manji (eds) *African Perspectives on China in Africa*. Nairobi and Oxford: Fahamu.

12 Daniel Large (2007) 'As the beginning ends: China's return to Africa', Patrick Burnett and Firoze Manji (eds) *African Perspectives on China in Africa*. Nairobi and Oxford: Fahamu.

13 Michelle Chan-Fishel (2007) 'Environmental impact: more of the same?', in Patrick Burnett and Firoze Manji (eds) *African Perspectives on China in Africa*. Nairobi and Oxford: Fahamu.

14 John Rocha (2007).

15 BBC (2006) 28 April <http://news.bbc.co.uk/2/hi/africa/4953588.stm>.

16 Chris Melville and Olly Owen (2005) 'China and Africa: a new era of "south-south cooperation"', Open Democracy, 8 July <http://www.opendemocracy.net/globalization-G8/south_2658.jsp>.

17 Chris Alden and Martyn Davies (2006) 'A profile of the operation of Chinese multinationals in Africa', *South African Journal of International Affairs*, 13(1): 84.

18 http://english.people.com.cn/200601/12/eng20060112_234894.html.

19 Mark Sobara (2006) *The Nation*, Nairobi, 14 April, quoted by Yang Lihua in 'Africa; a view from China', *South African Journal of International Affairs*, 13(1).

20 Alden and Davies (2006).

21 Quoted by Alden and Davies (2006), p. 91.

22 Reuters South Africa (2006) 'Samancor signs China chrome deals', 9 November <http://za.today. reuters.com/news/newsArticle.aspx?type=businessNews&storyID=2006-11-09T062122Z_01_BAN922845_ RTRIDST_0_OZABS-MINERALS-CHROME-SAMANCOR-20061109.XML>

23 Leni Wild and David Mepham (eds) (2006) *The New Sinosphere: China in Africa*, Institute for Public Policy Research, 51.

24 Alden and Davies (2006) p. 95.

25 China View (2006) 'HSBC banks on sustained growth', 17 October <http://news.xinhuanet.com/english/2006-10/17/content_5212967.htm>.

26 Leni Wild and David Mepham (2006).

27 Dorothy Guerrero (2006) 'China: beyond the growth figures', *The Globalist*, 21 February <2006http://www.theglobalist.com/DBWeb/printStoryId.aspx?StoryId=5095 >

28 People's Daily Online (2006) 'China facing employment crisis with 34.5 mln new job-seekers in next five years' <http://english.people.com.cn/200610/16/print20061016_312247.html>.

29 Richard McGregor (2006) 'China's poorest worse off after boom', *Financial Times*, 12 November <http://www.ft.com/cms/s/e28495ce-7988-11db-b257-0000779e2340.html>.

30 Pan Yue and Zhou Jigang (2006) 'The rich consume and the poor suffer the pollution', Chinadialogue, 27 October <http://www.chinadialogue.net/article/show/single/en/493--The-rich-consume-and-the-poor-suffer-the-pollution-?page=1#disscuss-bara%20chinese%20ecosocialist?>.

31 Peter Kwong (2006) 'China and the US are joined at the hip: the Chinese face of neoliberalism', *Counterpunch*, 7/8 October <http://www.counterpunch.org/kwong10072006.html>.

32 Sophie Beach (2006) 'China's New Left calls for a social alternative – Pankaj Mishra', China Digital Times, 13 October <http://chinadigitaltimes.net/2006/10/chinas_new_left_calls_for_a_social_lternative_pankaj_m.php>.

# SOUTH AFRICA'S COEGA COMPLEX – CHEAP ENERGY FOR INDUSTRY

**PATRICK BOND**

January 2007

The South African government is channelling Africa's largest-ever industrial subsidies into the Coega industrial zone complex and port, located in the country's fourth largest city, the Nelson Mandela Metropole (better known by its apartheid-era name, Port Elizabeth). Government proponents say Coega represents sound industrial and development policy, but a growing legion of critics are labelling it a grandiose and unworkable public investment scheme in a country that does not have resources to spare.

Aside from tailor-made infrastructure, including a 20-metre deep port, the key attraction of Coega for foreign investors is super-cheap energy. Following a year of frequent brownouts in the two largest metropolitan areas, Johannesburg and Cape Town, a fierce debate has erupted over the provision of discounted electricity to industrial users when citizens cannot get a dependable supply at any price. Mismanagement of the state electricity company, Eskom, in the course of its corporatisation, has interfered with a steady supply.

The main beneficiary of Coega's cheap energy, the Canadian firm Alcan, agreed in early December to a quarter-century power supply agreement from Eskom – the

> *a fierce debate has erupted over the provision of discounted electricity to industrial users when citizens cannot get a dependable supply at any price*

world's fourth-largest power company – at an extremely generous price, less than the $0.02 cents per hour that bulk industrial consumers pay. This is already the world's cheapest electricity, but Alcan insisted on the subsidy because of volatile commodity prices, a factor that has caused consternation in prior deals the South African government made with large mining houses and metals smelters such as BHP Billiton, the Anglo-American group and Mittal Steel.

Alcan and Eskom claim that the deal will bring job creation and foreign exchange earnings to the country. Using imported bauxite, Coega's $3 billion aluminum smelter could by 2014 produce 720,000 tons of the metal annually in one of the world's biggest smelters. Fewer than 1,000 permanent jobs will be created in the process, however.

Coega is one in a long list of post-apartheid mega-projects undertaken by the South African government. These include the Pebble Bed nuclear reactors (one of the first global deployments of a new nuclear energy technology that purports to offer new safety guarantees), the Lesotho Highlands water project (six vast dams under construction), which supplies Johannesburg with its water, and the 'Gautrain' elite fast rail network that will link Johannesburg, Pretoria and the country's largest airport. An impoverished South African majority, increasingly well organised and mobilised, is challenging these mega-projects and demanding instead that state resources be deployed to deliver basic services to the majority, on a more ecologically sustainable basis.

## The costs of corporate welfare

Coega's site will include a new port, container terminal and industrial development zone (IDZ), utilising vast public investments – at least $1.5 billion, including a $300 million tax break for Alcan – and enormous quantities of land, water and electricity. The new employment anticipated at the port/IDZ would be the most expensive, in terms of capital per job, of any major facility in Africa. Environmentally, the costs of the Coega projects in water consumption, air pollution, electricity usage and marine impacts are potentially immense.

The infrastructure under construction is unprecedented in Africa, and dwarfs the basic-needs development infrastructure required by deprived citizens of Mandela Metropole and across the Eastern Cape. Hence controversy has surrounded the decision -making process to construct the port and IDZ. Reports of conflicts of interest for key decision-makers cloud the project's governance. Coega was also initially meant to represent a key site at which European industrial firms involved in arms sales to South Africa could make 'offset' investments that would create jobs, so government could justify to the public its corruption-ridden $6 billion weapons purchase. These have not so far been forthcoming.

Socially, there are significant costs as well. Several hundred families have already been displaced to build Coega's infrastructure, and those in the area will bear the brunt of the environmental toll exacted by the project. The opportunity costs of Coega include as many as 10,000 jobs lost in economic sectors which either must close or cannot expand, including the existing salt works, mariculture, fisheries, agriculture and eco-tourism. Most importantly, community and environmental activists point to far better prospects for employment creation and socio-economic progress if resources were used elsewhere. Six years ago, the Mandela Metropole Sustainability Coalition proposed an alternative economic development scenario. The alternative strategy prioritises basic-needs infrastructure investment throughout the Eastern Cape and, at Coega, the development of state-supported eco-tourism and black-owned small-scale agriculture and mariculture.

---

*An impoverished South African majority, increasingly well organised and mobilised, is challenging these mega-projects and demanding instead that state resources be deployed to deliver basic services to the majority, on a more ecologically sustainable basis.*

---

Of the many subsidy components of Coega, civic groups find Eskom's new deal most worrying, given the persistent electricity shortage across South Africa and the problem of mass disconnections of poor people for whom electricity remains too expensive. Using roughly 1,300 megawatts, about 3 per cent of the country's total, Coega will be an enormous new drain, requiring expensive new transmission lines from Eskom's coal-fired generators 1,000 kilometres away.

Moreover, South Africa's carbon dioxide emissions are already running approximately 20 times higher than even the United States on the basis of per capita income. Ironically, Environment Minister Martinus van Schalkwyk returned triumphant from the November climate change treaty renegotiations in Nairobi, claiming that 'South Africa achieved most of its key objectives'. Those included promoting 'clean development mechanisms' (CDMs).

By bringing the vast 'ghost on the Coast' (the long-empty Coega's nickname) to life through the new subsidies, the national government will substantially increase carbon emissions. Yet because Alcan promises to use relatively energy efficient technologies, the market-oriented New York-based group Environmental Defense has suggested that Coega be considered worthy of CDM investments by large international polluters, which would permit them to continue present rates of emissions. In promoting these kinds of investments, Van Schalkvyk says that his government is sending 'a clear signal to carbon markets of our common resolve to secure the future of the Kyoto regime'. But there are vast problems with the new emissions trading system, and projects such as Coega show why this market should not be expanded in ways that generate new ecological problems without making a dent in overall emissions.

## Captive regulation and revolving doors

From the standpoint of meeting basic needs for electricity, South Africa's regulation of Eskom and municipal distributors has not been successful. This is not only because of an extremely weak performance by the initial national electricity regulator – Xolani Mkhwanazi, who subsequently became, tellingly, chief operating officer for BHP Billiton Aluminum Southern Africa – but also because government policy has increasingly imposed 'cost-reflective tariffs', as a 1995 document insisted. The key issue is whether all consumers must cover the costs of the electricity they use, or whether richer and industrial consumers pay higher rates to subsidise the poor.

The 1998 White Paper allowed for 'moderately subsidised tariffs' for poor domestic consumers. (White Papers are formal governmental policy statements.) But it also stated, 'cross-subsidies should have minimal impact on the price of electricity to con-

---

*Environmentally, the costs of the Coega projects*
*in water consumption, air pollution, electricity usage and*
*marine impacts are potentially immense.*

---

sumers in the productive sectors of the economy', meaning industrial users should not subsidise costs for poor residential consumers.

In addition to Mkhwanazi, the man responsible for Eskom's late-apartheid pricing – Mick Davis – left the parastatal's treasury to become the London-based operating head of Billiton. Davis took the post after former Finance Minister Derek Keys gave permission for an Afrikaner-controlled industrial company (Gencor) to expatriate vast assets in order to buy Billiton from Shell. After apartheid ended, Keys became chief executive of Billiton.

Ironically, the deals that gave Billiton, Anglo American and other huge corporations the world's lowest electricity prices came under attack in 2005 from Alec Erwin, the minister of public enterprises. The package Davis had given Billiton for smelters north of Durban and in Maputo, Mozambique, during the period when Eskom had extreme overcapacity, resulted in prices that often dropped below $0.01 per kilowatt hour, when world aluminium prices fell. (Most households pay five times that amount.)

Erwin reportedly insisted on lower 'financial-reporting volatility'. Because the amount the foreign companies pay for energy changes with the value of the rand, every time the rand changes value by 10 per cent, Eskom's wins or loses $300 million. Erwin said the utility should work to escape from existing contracts. From

Billiton's side, Mkhwanazi replied that any change to the current contracts could be 'a bit tricky for us. ... We would adopt a pragmatic approach and, who knows, perhaps there will even be some sweeteners in it for us.'

---

*The alternative economic development strategy prioritises basic-needs infrastructure investment throughout the Eastern Cape and, at Coega, the development of state-supported eco-tourism and black-owned small-scale agriculture and mariculture.*

---

But the allegedly new approach was not applied at Coega, where Erwin as trade and industry minister from 1996 to 2004 had led negotiations for a new smelter. According to the chief executive of the parastatal Industrial Development Corporation (IDC), Geoffrey Qhena, 'The main issue was the electricity price and that has been resolved. Alcan has put a lot of resources into this, which is why we are confident it will go ahead.'

Meanwhile, however, to operate a new smelter at Coega, lubricated by at least 15 per cent financing from the IDC, Alcan and other large aluminum firms were in the process of shutting European plants that produce 600,000 metric tonnes between 2006 and 2009, simply 'in search of cheaper power', according to industry analysts.

The main Alcan negotiator, 49-year-old Cynthia Carroll of the United States, was recognised for her skill in browbeating South African officials when in late 2006 she was named CEO-designate at Anglo American Corporation. Breaking the longstanding tradition, dating to the era of founder Ernest Oppenheimer, of giving the top job to insider elderly male candidates, Anglo's offer was seen as a way to better position the firm – South Africa's largest even though its financial headquarters since 1999 are in London – for further international metals deals.

## Coal-fired power, climate change and carbon trading

The state's decision to provide Alcan such vast subsidies at Coega comes amidst rising elite and popular consciousness about climate change problems. For years, global rulers have avoided action on $CO_2$ emissions, as reflected in October 2006 in Monterrey, in the wake of that year's St Petersburg summit of the G8 group of rich countries, which ignored climate change. In Monterrey, the G8's energy ministers were joined by 12 other major polluters, including South Africa, but again, no commitments were made to reduce greenhouse gas emissions.

Three weeks later, however, the British government released *The Stern Review: The Economics of Climate Change*, which estimates climate change costs of 5–20 per cent of global GDP at current warming rates. Former World Bank chief economist Nick Stern calls for demand-reduction of emissions-intensive products (the opposite of Coega), energy efficiency, avoiding deforestation and new low-carbon technology.

The key problem is that Stern and the establishment want many of these improvements to be financed via carbon trading. Likewise, in 2002, Princeton University researcher Nipun Vats and Environmental Defense – through its 'Partnership for Climate Action' relationship with French aluminum firm Pechiney (subsequently purchased by Alcan) – promoted Coega as eligible for subsidies under the CDM. Coega could receive such subsidies if it can show its technology is cleaner than existing aluminium suppliers, and in turn that the energy-savings smelter technology can only be profitably financed through 'additional' investment resources, using carbon trading mechanisms like the World Bank's Prototype Carbon Fund.

In November, Alcan said it would proceed with the $2.7 billion aluminium Coega smelter thanks to vast electricity subsidies from Eskom. Within days, University of Cape Town Environmental Studies Professor Richard Fuggle – the country's most respected environmentalist – attacked the increase in $CO_2$ emissions due to Coega in his retirement speech. He described Van Schalkwyk as a 'political lightweight' who is 'unable to press for environmental considerations to take precedence over development'.

According to Fuggle, 'It is rather pathetic that van Schalkwyk has expounded the virtues of South Africa's 13 small projects to garner carbon credits under the Kyoto Protocol's CDM, but has not expressed dismay at Eskom selling 1,360 megawatts a year of coal-derived electricity to a foreign aluminium company. We already have one of the world's highest rates of carbon emissions per dollar of GDP. Adding the carbon that will be emitted to supply power to this single factory will make us number one on this dubious league table.'

## Civil society begins to react

In Mandela Metropole, emerging resistance to Coega's guzzling of water and power will add to existing popular unrest. In South Africa during 2004–05, the police counted more than 5,800 protests against government, possibly the highest per-person rate in the world. In China, with 1.3 billion people, there were 87,000 mainly rural protests, while South Africa's population is 45 million.

Thirty years ago, in the wake of the Soweto uprising near Johannesburg, the revitalised anti-apartheid social movements known as civic associations were founded in Port Elizabeth's impoverished townships, thanks in part to the legacy of black consciousness and community empowerment activist Steve Biko, who was killed by the city's police in 1979.

## Stop economic partnership agreements

June 2006

Beyond what is required of African countries by the World Trade Organisation, economic partnership agreements (EPAs) have been set up between the European Union (EU) and African, Caribbean and Pacific countries (ACP) in order to enable Europe to have market access to goods and services in Africa. These negotiations, which began in 2002, are meant to promote sustainable development and contribute to poverty eradication in the ACP countries through the liberalisation of trade and tariffs.

But critics, including those academics and activists who form the Global Call for Action to Stop EPAs campaign, argue that these 'partnerships' are in fact unequal: the EU has overwhelming economic and political power and as such, can impose its interests, agenda and stipulations on ACP countries, which as a whole are fragile, both politically and economically, and dependent to a large extent on external funders. This vulnerability has the potential to increase poverty and debt and destabilise the economies of these nations.

Critics argue that these EPAs conspire to de-industrialise African countries, simply making them suppliers of raw materials and ensuring their markets are wholly dependent on Europe, which inhibits their already limited capacity, reports Third World Network Africa.

That EPA negotiations are taking place away from any public monitoring means that the large civil society base that has assembled around this issue has had little say in the discussion. Civil society organisations argue that EPAs will have negative effects, leading to deeper inequalities, greater unemployment, the loss of livelihoods, insecurity of food and other resources and will undermine social and human rights. They call for the EU and ACP negotiators to affirm the principles of non-reciprocity, protect ACP producers, reverse trade and investment liberalisation, and perhaps most importantly, allow that alternatives be found for ACP countries to pursue their own development strategies that work best for them.

**Sources**

'EPAs – Endless Poverty in Africa' <http://twnafrica.org/atn/campaigns/day4.htm>

'Global Call for Action to Stop EPAs – campaign statement' <http://www.liberationafrique.org/article.php3?id_article=1213>

**Further reading**

Charles Abugre (2005) 'Economic partnership agreements and putting development first', Pambazuka News 216 <http://www.pambazuka.org/en/category/features/28901>

Demba Moussa Dembele (2005) 'Meeting Africa's human development needs and the failure of EPAs', Pambazuka News 216 <http://www.pambazuka.org/en/category//28905>

Liz Dodd (2005) 'Growing resistance to EPAs', Pambazuka News 216 <http://www.pambazuka.org/en/category/features/28903>

Richard Kamidza (2005) 'Predictions for the economic partnership agreements negotiations: EU=1, ACP=0', Pambazuka News 216 <http://www.pambazuka.org/en/category/features/28907>

Bibiane Mbaye (2005) 'Economic partnership agreements or broken partnerships? The case of West Africa', Pambazuka News 216 <http://www.pambazuka.org/en/category/features/28902>

Pambazuka News (2005) 'Economic partnership agreements: territorial conquest by economic means?', Pambazuka News 216 <http://www.pambazuka.org/en/issue/216>

Pambazuka News (2005) 'Trade terms: a guide to EPAs', Pambazuka News 216 <http://www.pambazuka.org/en/category/features/28908>

Karin Ulmer (2005) 'Negotiating a fair deal: are trade agreements with the EU beneficial to women?', Pambazuka News 216 <http://www.pambazuka.org/en/category/features/28906>

Christina Weller (2005) 'Learning the rules: the WTO and EPAs', Pambazuka News 216 <http://www.pambazuka.org/en/category/features/28904>

Twenty years later, the assistant city engineer for hydraulics wrote a blunt memo about the prospects for imposing a redistributive tariff to help poor consumers through cross-subsidisation, funded by higher prices paid by large industrial users: if such a plan 'were to be implemented for industry, Coega would not go ahead'.

The redistributive scheme subsequently adopted by the city does not assure low-income citizens basic electricity and water access. In other words, the perceived need to pump cheap water and electricity into Coega industries is likely to sabotage the government's objectives of social justice, public health, and economic growth via municipal services.

In all these respects, say critics, the Coega port and IDZ exacerbate the apartheid economic legacy of division, marginalisation and grandiose, unworkable public-investment schemes. Such ventures were traditionally grounded not in a logic of development, but instead reflected the power of special interest groups.

Civil society resistance to this sort of maldistribution is already quite advanced, but often takes the form of illegal reconnections after prolific disconnections by municipalities and Eskom. To alter policy decisions, what is needed is a more sustained campaign for radically new industrial policies as well as tough state regulation of emissions. It may be inspired by the case of Coega, which stands out as a beacon of irresponsibility and corporate welfare.

This article was originally commissioned by Multinational Monitor (http://www.multinationalmonitor.org) and is reproduced here with kind permission of the author.

Notes

1 See K. Horta (1996) 'Making the earth rumble: the Lesotho-South African water connection', Multinational Monitor, 17(5).

Lessons from the slave trade

# A STORY OF THE ATLANTIC SLAVE TRADE

**MANU HERBSTEIN**

February 2006

Manu Herbstein's first novel, *Ama, a Story of the Atlantic Slave Trade*, recently published in South Africa by Picador Africa, won the 2002 Commonwealth Writers Best First Book Prize. Set in the late 18th century, it tells the story of a young woman who is captured and enslaved in the West African savannah and transported to Brazil. Here, Herbstein reflects on the historical background to his novel and some of its contemporary implications.

Some 40 years ago the distinguished British professor of history, Hugh Trevor-Roper, told a BBC audience: 'Perhaps in the future, there will be some African history to teach. But, at present there is none: there is only the history of the Europeans in Africa. The rest is darkness...'

In 1772 or thereabouts, Ama is quietly going about her business at her home in the West African savannah. She is about to be overwhelmed by waves, tsunamis, of history, African and European history, of which she is almost entirely ignorant. Living, as she is, in a quiet, rural, pre-industrial society, we may excuse her ignorance. Given Trevor-Roper's profession and status, his ignorance was inexcusable. Regrettably, except among specialists, that ignorance of African history remains widespread today.

I am not an historian. Indeed, I am not any sort of academic. So I ask you to approach the potted historical background which I am going to offer you with some reserve. For one-stop access to the texts I have used you might like to look at the book's companion website, www.ama.africatoday.com. One further caveat: you should bear in mind that much of our knowledge of West African history is derived from European sources, which may be distorted by their unwitting ideological baggage.

Returning to my metaphor of tsunamis, what I am going to do is to describe briefly the dry land on which Ama (or Nandzi, to give her her birthname) stands as the novel opens and then, again briefly, to describe each of the several waves of history which threaten to engulf her: the histories, if they can be separated, of Dagbon, Asante and Europe; and of gold, kola and sugar.

## Human settlement in the West African Sudan

The peopling of West Africa began, perhaps, towards the end of the last ice age, say around 7,000 years ago, during a period when the Sahara was green. Early immigration would have been slow and the numbers small.

Let me now slip into the historical present tense.

Over the course of many centuries the Western Sudan, the savannah country to the south of the Sahara, becomes populated. Many people live in acephalous societies, some of which, beloved of anthropologists, still exist. Ama's people, who call themselves Bekpokpam, but are known to others as Konkomba, are one such. They develop, as one might expect, a culture which is intimately connected with their physical environment. So, to give just one example, their religious practices are concerned with protection from a sometimes hostile climate and with encouragement of fertility, both of the soil and of their womenfolk.

History is recorded, by and large, to reflect the glory of strong rulers. Since the Konkomba have no strong rulers, they preserve little of their history. What they remember, principally, is their 'tsunami,' when they were overwhelmed by mounted invaders from the north.

## Dagbon

The invaders call themselves Dagomba; their state is known as Dagbon.

In the 16th century or earlier, perhaps, the ancestors of the Dagomba live in the vicinity of Lake Chad. They are troubled by the depredations of the 'white men from the desert,' that is, Touareg raiders; and decide to migrate. For a generation or more they wander within the bend of the Niger River, surviving from the proceeds of occasional brigandry. In due course they settle in the vicinity of what is now the city of Tamale, in northern Ghana and, later, towards the Togo border to the east, where they establish their capital, Yendi. This is the country of the Konkomba, some of whom submit to and are absorbed by the invaders while others stubbornly retain their own separate identity.

In the early 18th century, through the influence of Hausa traders, Dagbon adopts Islam. The Hausa traders arrive each year, after the rains, in search of kola.

## Kola

In early times, the tropical forest bars migration from the savannah down to the Atlantic coast; however the Volta River offers one way through. So we have a populated coastal strip separated from the savannah by a 200km-wide belt of forest.

The natural environment of the tropical forest is a major factor in determining how, and how quickly, it is penetrated by man. The canopy of the forest is so dense that little light penetrates to the ground. The vegetation at ground level is consequently light. Adventurous hunters in search of game are the first humans to enter the forest. In due course some of them establish small settlements. The trees are enormous and closely spaced. Even after the introduction of iron tools, perhaps 2,000 years ago, it requires a great input of labour to clear areas for agriculture. The problems are exacerbated by the poor quality of tropical soils. After only three or four crops the nutrients are exhausted and decreasing yields force the farmer to clear new areas.

> *Every person who lives in one of the countries*
> *of the Atlantic rim carries within him or her, the marks*
> *of the slave trade, like some unrecognised gene. We are all*
> *the descendants of those who suffered and those who,*
> *in one way or another, benefitted. The Atlantic slave trade*
> *is the bedrock upon which the mighty edifice*
> *of globalisation has been constructed.*

Powerful economic incentives are needed to make settlement viable. Of these there are two: kola and gold.

The kola tree is indigenous to these forests. Its seeds fall to the ground, where they may be collected. The kola 'nut' is a pink and white seed about the size of a thumb. It has a mildly narcotic effect and is reputed to stave off hunger and thirst. Its economic value stems from the fact that Islam does not prohibit its use. In order to realise this value, labour is required to clear the ground beneath the kola trees, to gather the seeds and to transport them in head-loaded baskets to entrepôts beyond the northern extent of the forest. The market for kola encompasses the entire Muslim world.

## Gold

From around the eighth century of our era, the kingdoms of the western Sudan, first ancient Ghana, and then Mali and Songhai, are the most important suppliers of gold to the Mediterranean, exporting, on average, a ton of gold across the Sahara each year. West African gold makes a vital contribution to the monetisation of the medieval Mediterranean economy.

School children in West Africa learn of Mansa Musa, the king of Mali who died in 1337. In making the hajj, Mansa Musa takes with him 100 camel-loads of gold and distributes so much of the precious metal in Cairo and Mecca that the bottom drops out of the market.

The trans-Saharan trade in gold reaches its peak around the end of the 17th century. In due course, the local alluvial and surface deposits become depleted and the Malians send exploratory missions throughout West Africa in search of new supplies. They discover a rich source in the forest of what is now the modern state of Ghana. By that time there is competition from European buyers at the coast.

The kola trade requires labour; so does the mining of gold. And so, too, does the establishment of agriculture, to support the miners and porters and the new aristocrats who are the descendants of the first settlers. Guns and powder purchased from the Europeans at the coast offer the means of obtaining that labour.

By the second half of the 17th century, gradual development of the forest economy has reached a level at which the establishment of a large centralised state is a viable project.

## The Europeans: Portuguese, Dutch and British

During the period 1400–1600, Europe, emerging from the lethargy of the Middle Ages, witnesses the renewal of nationalism as well as the political transformation from feudalism to nation states. The exploration of the Atlantic leads to the establishment of Europe's commercial empires and, in due course, to the industrial revolution. The Atlantic slave trade plays an important role in the growth of the European economy.

The Portuguese know that there is gold in West Africa: they aim to bypass the Saharan trade and get access to the gold through the back door. In 1482, five years before Bartholomew Diaz rounds the Cape, the Portuguese aristocrat Dom Diego d'Azambuja arrives, with several ships, at a village on the coast of what is now Ghana. His ships are laden with building materials and after negotiating with the local chief, he starts to build a brick and stone castle, which the Portuguese name Elmina. By 1486 d'Azambuja's castle of St. George is substantially complete.

St. George's Castle at Elmina is the oldest surviving European building in the tropics. It is a useful symbolic marker of the beginning of the process of the worldwide expansion of European power which we now call globalisation.

In 1637, 15 years before Van Riebeeck's arrival at the Cape, the Dutch expel the Portuguese from Elmina Castle. They are to stay there for 235 years, until 1872, when, seeing neither economic nor political advantage in remaining, they sell the building, by then much extended, to the British.

I first visited Elmina Castle in 1961 or '62. At the time it was being used as a training college for the Ghana police force and was not open to the public. I was living and working at Cape Coast, some 15km to the east of Elmina. One of the small colony of South African schoolteachers there, Manilal Moodley (who was later to become

71

Zimbabwe's first ombudsman), was friendly with the commander of the police college. Mani took me with him on my first visit to the castle. I was totally ignorant of its significance and that of the many other slave castles which line the Ghanaian coast. I have to admit that I remained in that state of ignorance for many years. I am comforted by the thought that I was not alone in this respect. My sister, the distinguished Ghanaian novelist, Ama Ata Aidoo, told me many, many years later: 'I grew up in the shadow of those castles, but no one ever told me what they were or what they meant.'

The first chapter of *Ama* which I wrote is set in Elmina Castle and is based upon a story which the tourist guides still tell. It is now chapter 13. It had the advantage that, unlike the rest of the book, it required little research.

## Asante

We return to the forest.

In the year 1700 Nana Osei Tutu establishes the Asante Confederacy, Asanteman, with Kumase as its capital. Its economy is based upon the export of kola and gold. It sells gold to the Dutch in exchange for guns. It uses the guns to expand its empire by conquest. Conquest of the surrounding states provides it with the labour it needs to mine the gold and gather and export the kola. It sells the captives in excess of its labour requirements to the Dutch and the English at the coast.

Asante imposes strict limitations upon the activities of foreign traders within its territory. The Europeans are confined to small areas around their castles and forts on the

*Has the time not come for Africa to set up its own commission, a Commission on the State of the African Diaspora, a commission tasked with the identification and exposure of all discrimination against people of African descent, whatever their nationality, in all countries; and the elimination of all forms of such discrimination?*

coast. The kola markets are on the north bank of the Volta River, which the Hausa traders are not permitted to cross. In order to consolidate its control of the kola trade routes, Asante invades Dagbon, first in 1744 and again in 1772. It stations a consul in Yendi, the Dagomba capital, to ensure delivery of an annual tribute. The tribute comprises so many sheep and goats, so many pieces of cotton cloth and so many of silk cloth – and 500 slaves. Asante concedes that none of the slaves will be Dagomba. So every year the Ya Na, the Dagomba ruler, sends out raiding parties to capture slaves for delivery to Kumase. Many of the captives are Konkomba. Nandzi, later to be known as Ama, is one. The labour of slaves makes a substantial contribution to the Asante economy. However, the slavery practised by the Asante differs so fundamentally from the chattel slavery of the Europeans that it hardly makes sense to use the same word for the two practices. In Asante, slaves are absorbed into the population within a generation and became all but full citizens. Indeed, Asante law encourages integration by prohibiting the public disclosure of the origins of any citizen.

By the end of the 18th century Asante has established political supremacy over the territories that comprise most of modern Ghana and east-central and south-eastern Côte d'Ivoire. It is a sophisticated, complex and wealthy state. It maintains large monetary reserves including its treasury's great chest, which when full contains some 200,000 ounces, say 5,000 or 6,000kg, of gold.

## Europe and Africa

It is instructive to consider some aspects of the state of Europe at this time, the last quarter of the 18th century. Britain, emerging as the pre-eminent power, serves as an example.

In 1775 George III signs an order releasing from bondage the women and children, many of them younger than eight years old, who work in British coal and salt mines in conditions not much removed from slavery. The following year the British Parliament debates (and rejects) the first motion to outlaw slavery in Britain and her colonies. Another 32 years are to pass before the slave trade is outlawed and yet another 27 before the practice of slavery itself becomes illegal.

In Britain at this time, Roy Porter tells us, criminals are publicly whipped, pilloried, and hanged; until 1777 Jacobites' heads are spiked on Temple Bar. In the England of 1800 there are some 200 capital offences. Many specify death for small-scale theft such as pick-pocketing goods worth more than a shilling. The penalty for poaching is often transportation.

The British seldom bathe. Before cottons become cheap, clothes are difficult to wash; children in particular are often sewn into theirs for the duration of the winter. The use of underclothes is recent and not widespread. Chamber pots are provided in the dining-room sideboards of the wealthy, to save interrupting the conversation of the gentlemen. Food hygiene is no better than personal hygiene. The streets are full of the excrement of humans and horses. This is a world lit by candles and rush-lights.

There is not a single bathing establishment in London in 1800. By way of contrast, Thomas Astley, writing in 1745 of the 'Gold Coast Negroes, their Persons, Character and Dress', says: 'They are very careful in washing their bodies morning and evening, and anointing them with palm-oil.'

73

In 1771, 107 slave ships sail from Liverpool, transporting 50,000 slaves from Africa. Colonial trade at the time amounts to one third of British commerce. In the 1780s British slave traders top the international league, carrying more slaves from Africa than those of any other country. By 1790 British capitalists have invested some £70 million in the West Indian sugar economy, an economy which is based almost entirely on slave labour. During the 18th century British slave-traders transport a million and a half Africans. The slave trade is a vital pillar in the 18th century economy of the port city of Liverpool, underpinning the growth in its trade and shipping. It is not surprising that Liverpool merchants are amongst the most vocal opponents of legislation outlawing the slave trade in 1807.

## Sugar and the slave trade

What was the slave trade all about? Here is one banal, if partial, explanation. In their voyages of discovery the Europeans found and took home three beverages: cocoa, coffee and tea, all of them bitter to the taste. This is what accounts for the dramatic rise in European consumption of sugar (in Britain, for example, 200,000 pounds in 1690, 5,000,000 pounds in 1760.) Add tobacco, rice and cotton, and the labour needed to cultivate these crops in the tropics, and there you have it.

## *Ama* and the legacy of the slave trade

The historian John Hunwick has written that he would 'like to see slavery viewed from the perspective of the Africans who were victims of it.' But those Africans are long dead and have left hardly any documentary records of their experience. Who will speak for them?

The French historian Claude Meillassoux writes: 'While the slave trade devastated the peasantry who saw their children, and especially their daughters, taken away by brigands or armed bands to be sold to dealers, it enriched the agents and traders in the towns as well as the nobility, the battle-hardened soldiers and the sycophants attached to the royal courts. By a perversion of memory, the sumptuousness of the plundering kings has left its mark on the area in its remembrance of the flourishing slave trade and the glories of the past, while the memory of their peasant victims has been effaced by their poverty.'

In *Ama*, I set out to recreate such a memory.

Hugh Thomas writes: 'Any historian of the slave trade is conscious of a large gap in (the) picture. For the slave remains an unknown warrior, invoked by moralists on both sides of the Atlantic, recalled now in museums in one-time slave ports from Liverpool to Elmina, but all the same unspeaking, and therefore remote and elusive.'

I have attempted, in *Ama*, to give that unknown warrior a voice.

It is not for me to judge whether I have succeeded. The late Paul Hair, also a historian of the slave trade, believed that: 'The feelings and sufferings of the slaves are partly unimaginable…Standard descriptions which concentrate on those aspects easily comprehensible to modern middle class sentiment cannot tell the whole story.' Perhaps he was right.

Four hundred years is a long time in human history, as we perceive it. It is less than 400 years since the disembarkation of Jan van Riebeck changed the course of South African history.

The trans-Atlantic slave trade lasted for 400 years. African slaves were sold in Lisbon as early as 1441. It was 1850 before the slave trade became illegal in Brazil and 1888 before slavery itself was finally made unlawful in that country. During those 400 years European and American ships forcibly transported some 12 million African men, women and children to the far shores of the Atlantic. Millions more died on the journey to the coast, in the dungeons and barracoons in which they were assembled and in the course of the notorious Middle Passage.

By accident or good fortune, the Atlantic slavers by-passed South Africa: they took many slaves from Angola and some from Mozambique but few from this country. We have, of course, our own story of the slave trade; but it is a different story.

I believe that *Ama* is an important book. In saying that, I make no claims for its literary merit: that is for others to judge. However, with the exception of perhaps two other somewhat obscure texts, both out of print, it is to the best of my knowledge the only attempt to tell this story from the point of view of an enslaved African, using the results of historical research now available to us. It is a story which should perhaps have been written by a Ghanaian. But West Africa is only now slowly beginning to emerge from a long period of collective amnesia regarding the slave trade. The damage to the psyche caused by the slave trade is buried deep in the individual and collective subconscious. One historian traces the institutionalised corruption endemic in West Africa back to practices developed during the period of the slave trade.

The situation on the other side of the Atlantic is quite different. When black pilgrims from the Americas visit the slave dungeons at Elmina and Cape Coast Castles, they are often overwhelmed by the experience and emerge tear-stained and emotionally drained. Many of them carry the pain of their families' histories within them. It is transmitted from generation to generation. And the reason is not far to seek. From Argentina to Canada, in Brazil, Columbia, Costa Rica, Guatemala, Honduras, Nicaragua, Peru, Uruguay, even Venezuela and, some say, even in Cuba, the descendants of African slaves are socially and economically disadvantaged; many suffer from chronic poverty and experience discrimination in every field. In the United States, the issue of slavery is one which few whites are at ease discussing with their black compatriots and vice versa. This is just one symptom of a deep and hardly recognised malaise in that country. Until the US, and in particular its educational system, comes to terms with the fact that it was constructed on a foundation of the gross abuse of generations of unwilling African immigrants, not to speak of the genocide inflicted upon its native inhabitants, that country will not sleep easy.

And what of Europe? Every person who lives in one of the countries of the Atlantic rim carries within him or her, the marks of the slave trade, like some unrecognised gene. We are all the descendants of those who suffered and those who, in one way or another, benefited. The Atlantic slave trade is the bedrock upon which the mighty edifice of globalisation has been constructed.

We are diminished by our failure to confront this history. So long as a single person of African descent suffers discrimination on account of his descent, all Africans are diminished, Nelson Mandela is diminished, Thabo Mbeki is diminished, John Kuffuor, president of Ghana, is diminished. And it is not only blacks, not only Africans who are diminished: all human beings are diminished, we are all diminished.

Some Englishman has had the chutzpah to establish a commission on Africa. Has the time not come for Africa to set up its own commission, a Commission on the State of the African Diaspora, a commission tasked with the identification and exposure of all discrimination against people of African descent, whatever their nationality, in all countries; and the elimination of all forms of such discrimination? Perhaps we need an international Truth and Reconciliation Commission, charged with bringing into the open the great harm the people of Europe and their descendants worldwide have inflicted on other peoples in the course of their conquest of the planet. That might achieve some sort of catharsis which might lead us to a new world based on human solidarity rather than greed, patronage and charity.

In March 2007, I predict an epidemic of dislocated shoulders amongst members of the British establishment. This will be the consequence of their attempts to pat themselves on the back in celebrating the bicentenary of legislation making the slave trade unlawful. Would it be too ambitious to aim to celebrate in 2034, 200 years after slavery was made illegal in the British Empire, the total elimination of its psychological and material effects? My hope is that the publication of this novel might make a small contribution to that end.

# SLAVERY AIN'T DEAD,
# IT'S MANUFACTURED IN LIBERIA'S RUBBER

**ROBTEL NEAJAI PAILEY**

May 2007

While England celebrates its 200th anniversary of the abolition of the slave trade, Robtel Pailey describes how plantation workers in Liberia are trapped in a time warp of monumental proportions.

## Historical background

In the early 1820s, Liberia was transformed into a land of exile for repatriated American slaves and declared Africa's first republic in 1847. In fact, the country was a proverbial refuge from the dehumanising, deplorable conditions of chattel slavery in the United States. So any mention of the word 'plantation' should have Liberians visibly shuddering from the historical legacy that many of its descendants endured.

Ironically enough, a recent development suggests that Liberia itself has served as a breeding ground for modern day slavery disguised in the form of what some would call indentured servitude for the American corporation, Firestone Tire and Rubber Company. The country has been embroiled in an asymmetrical relationship with the rubber giant since the corporation first landed on the shores of the country in 1926.

The history of Firestone in Liberia is revealing. In 1926, the company signed a concession agreement with the government of Liberia for a period of 99 years. That agreement covered 1,000,000 acres of land, leased for six cents per acre for a total annual price of US$60,000.

Large sectors of the indigenous population were displaced to pave the way for setting up Firestone's largest plantation in Harbel. Even in the company's infancy, Liberians were recruited to provide forced labour to harvest and cultivate the rubber trees, after which they engaged in 'tapping,' the labour-intensive act of using primitive tools to ease raw latex out of rubber trees for export. Labourers were initially conscripted at gunpoint.

Since 1926, Firestone has allegedly relied on forced labour, involuntary servitude, recklessness, negligence in hiring and supervision, unjust enrichment and unfair business practices. Many of the descendants of those labourers serve as plaintiffs in a civil action suit against Firestone today.

Clear violations of the law prompted a legal complaint in November 2005 against Bridgestone Corporation and Bridgestone Firestone North American Tire. The case was filed by the International Labour Rights Fund (ILRF), a member of the Stop Firestone Campaign: an advocacy coalition launched in 2005 to highlight Firestone's exploitative undermining of Liberian labour laws.

> *It is what I imagined the American south*
> *to have looked like during the centuries of*
> *chattel slavery in the United States.*

The plaintiffs brought their case to the US because the Liberian judicial system has been eroded in the mire of civil breakdown during more than 15 years of civil war and strife. The class action suit was lodged against the American company for violations of child labour laws, cruel and unusual labour practices, and environmental degradation. Practices, plaintiffs claim, are no different from the moment the plantation opened. The lawsuit states:

> The plantation workers are stripped of rights, they are isolated, they are at the mercy of Firestone for everything from food to health care to education, they risk expulsion and certain starvation if they raise even minor complaints, and the company makes wilful use of this situation to exploit these workers as they have since 1926.

The 35 plaintiffs either have been or are currently child labourers on the company's rubber plantation in Liberia. They describe their lives as 'trapped in poverty and coercion'. The case is ongoing.

## Modern day slavery

While England celebrates its 200th anniversary of the abolition of the slave trade, plantation workers in Liberia are trapped in a time warp of monumental proportions. They exist in the parallel universe of multinational corporate checkmate, where the prize goes to the highest exploiter. Firestone has been playing the chess pieces of Liberia's rubber slaves since the concession agreement was signed in 1926.

Rubber is Liberia's largest export, and Firestone its largest international corporate exploiter – or rather employer – to date. The country and its people have paid a high price for the asymmetrical relationship. In 2005, despite a surge of civil dissent and democratic outcries, Liberia's transitional government signed another concession agreement to lease the land for an extra 37 years of rubber slavery: for 50 cents per acre, a 'hike up' from the original leasing agreement.

According to a recent report published by the Save My Future Foundation, Firestone exported 167,165 tonnes of rubber between 2000 and 2003. The price of rubber reaches astronomical highs today at US$486 per tonne. In the measurement of trade regulations at present, Firestone is receiving US$81,242,190 from its production in Liberia. All of the rubber produced in Liberia is sent to the United States for processing into tyres and other materials. No processing, manufacturing, or other value-added production is done in Liberia.

## Today's plantation workers

I visited the Firestone Rubber plantation for the first time in December 2006 while on a research fact-finding mission. I decided to visit the sprawling modern day encampment I had heard so many horror stories about. It is what I imagined the American south to have looked like during the centuries of chattel slavery in the United States, with the hustle bustle activity of plantation life and the accompanying strokes of exploitation.

As my brother-in-law, Christopher Pabai, and I pulled into the 1,000,000 acre – and constantly expanding – plantation, we were welcomed by an ungodly stench of rotten cheese, the kind that has been drenched in burning oil, steamrolled on a conveyor belt, and neatly packaged for non-human consumption. That is what raw latex smells like when it is being processed. Rather than wearing masks to protect their noses from the assault, the plantation workers ingest the foul stench day in and day out.

A slender five foot three, Emmanuel B. is a 30-year-old slave whose piercing brown eyes tell unspeakable truths. He is not the kind of slave we are used to seeing in the collective imagination of 19th century plantations in the Deep South of the United States. No, Emmanuel is a modern slave in 21st century post-conflict Liberia. Firestone Tire and Rubber Company is his unyielding master.

Like many workers on Firestone's largest rubber plantation, Emmanuel was born in Harbel, has lived in Harbel all his life, and will most likely waste away in Harbel. Previously a student in Gbarnga, Emmanuel has ambitions to return to school. But those are pie in the sky dreams considering his family has no means of supporting him. He was gracious enough to demonstrate what a tapper does from sun-up to midmorning.

As Westerners drive around in their heavy-duty SUVs, propelled by another type of black gold, Firestone tyres, Emmanuel wakes up at the crack of dawn to tap raw latex from 800 rubber trees daily. His clothes are tattered, and his shoulders covered in red puss-infected blisters from carrying buckets suspended from an iron pole to the Firestone processing plant two miles from his tapping site. For Emmanuel and his fellow tappers, a 5 a.m. start is the only means of filling their daily quota. If workers do not fill their quotas, their wages are reduced by half. Some have even begun to use their children to complete the Herculean task.

Labourers work 12–15 hour days, then must enlist the help of their families (including young children and wives) to complete a daily quota in order to ensure a weekly wage. No days off, no paid holidays, no sick leave. The children and their families toil on the plantation by day, and return to the squalor of primitive living conditions at night with no electricity or running water.

Firestone blames the country's more than a decade long civil war for the breakdown of infrastructure. Yet members of the Firestone clan aided and abetted the rebel leader-turned president Charles Taylor so as to avoid damage to the plantation when the war raged on. Some of Taylor's rebel armies were even stationed at Harbel, enjoying the fruits of their fellow countrymen's literal blood, sweat and tears.

The level of poverty in Liberia is so astonishing that people flock to the plantation for a mere pittance. The average tapper generates US$900 monthly for the company yet receives barely a tenth of that as compensation from Firestone once fees and serv-

> *No days off, no paid holidays, no sick leave.*
> *The children and their families toil on the*
> *plantation by day, and return to the squalor*
> *of primitive living conditions at night with*
> *no electricity or running water.*

ices are deducted from wages. As a result, the tappers slog for a mere US$3.19 a day. After having worked for Firestone for over 50 years, some retired plantation workers apparently collect less than US$50 a month in pension earnings.

Aside from dealing with the poverty of indentured servitude, Firestone labourers must contend with health-related infirmities. The tappers expose their eyes to the potentially blinding latex, applying dangerous pesticides and fertilisers to the rubber trees. The raw latex from the rubber trees is fatal when applied to the eyes, as there have been countless reported cases of workers suffering from permanent eye damage due to exposure. They are forced to carry 35kg buckets overflowing with the collected latex quota of the day. Unschooled about the dangers of the products they are handling, the workers know not to ask for safety equipment. Many of the tappers, like Emmanuel, have severe scars and bone and muscle abnormalities as a result of the tapping.

## Child labour violations and environmental degradation

The deliberate and strategic use of children is against international laws including International Labour Office conventions, and American and Liberian labour laws.

Yet a shameful phenomenon in the Firestone scheme is its implied support of child labour. Workers live in dilapidated mud huts and are forced to seek the aid of their children in the strenuous and dangerous task of extracting latex from rubber trees. Most of the children are working on the plantations instead of attending school. The few who do, go to substandard schools in dilapidated conditions.

Firestone claims that it provides free education to the children of its workers, but in actuality the workers must pay an income tax automatically deducted from their monthly wages to cover the costs of so-called educational expenses.

Firestone's plantation workers and their children toil under the same slave-like conditions they have endured for the past 80 years. The children's labour usually includes cutting trees with sharp tools, applying pesticides by hand, and hauling two buckets

*The entire scenario represents a microcosm of inequitable trade rules benefitting large Western corporations that exploit raw material within the developing world, leaving the indigenous people with environmental spills, physical ailments and broken morale.*

on a pole, each filled with more than 30kg of latex. Every day, these child labourers have to work long hours and are thus denied the right to basic education. Access to the company-run schools is further impeded, as parents must present a costly birth certificate in order to register their children.

Violation of child labour laws is only one among a long list of indictments against Firestone. According to Friends of the Earth USA, discharge from the company's rubber processing plant has contaminated the adjacent Farmington River and other waterways, killing once vibrant ecosystems and polluting communities that depend on river water for drinking, bathing, and fishing.

Furthermore, plantation workers are exposed to toxic chemicals and compounds on a daily basis while tapping. The merciless exploitation of Liberia's people and natural resources by Firestone is directly linked to the nation's impoverishment as the raw materials produced in Liberia are sent elsewhere for processing, thereby shutting out the possibility of added value.

## Political responses and the reconstruction agenda

The ILRF, along with its Stop Firestone Coalition partners, demands that Firestone: provides workers with basic rights, including a living wage and the freedom of association; ends all child and forced labour and assigns achievable quotas; adopts health and safety standards; stops exposing workers to toxic compounds and chemicals; improves housing, schools, and health care centres to provide safe and comfortable facilities; ensures public disclosure of revenue and all types of foreign investment contracts; stops releasing chemicals into the environment and redresses all environmental damage; and publicly discloses the identity and quantity of all toxic compounds that it releases or transports.

Liberia's minister of labour, Kofi Woods, a long-time human rights activist and lawyer and a major catalyst for the Stop Firestone Campaign, has been in rounds of renegotiation sessions with Firestone representatives recently in Washington DC. Because of his list of demands – which are reminiscent of the Stop Firestone Coalition demands – Firestone representatives stormed out of the meetings in March 2007.

Woods and his cohorts are what African legislators should be like: uncompromising and unyielding when it comes to corporate social and ethical responsibility. Liberia's post-conflict reconstruction agenda will be null and void without a reconfiguration of the concession agreement with Firestone. After all, any post-war scheme involves a drastic revving up of the national economy. Given Firestone's economic entrenchment in Liberia, it will need to refashion how it deals with Liberian workers, thereby increasing employee profit margins. If a processing plant were built in Liberia, it could revolutionise the way rubber is used within a continent in dire need of manufactured goods – such as condoms in the heyday of Bush's conservative HIV/Aids funding policies.

## Inequitable trade and corporate takeover

In March 2007, the Firestone Tire and Rubber Company, a subsidiary of the Japan-based Bridgestone Corporation, won the Public Eye Global Ward for its social and ecological sins that are demonstrating the shady side of pure profit-oriented globalisation. The award was bestowed upon Firestone precisely because of the slave-like conditions on the plantation in Liberia.

The entire scenario represents a microcosm of inequitable trade rules benefiting large Western corporations that exploit raw material within the developing world, leaving the indigenous people with environmental spills, physical ailments and broken morale. The Firestone case in Liberia is a microcosm of American corporate takeover and a flagrant disregard of indigenous rights. It is an extension of the transatlantic slave trade, and should be exposed as such.

History challenges us to stay on a forward moving dialectic of change. The Firestone example shows us that an ironic distortion of that dialectic is taking place right under our noses. Slavery is not dead, it is manufactured in the rubber we use daily. We owe it to Emmanuel and his comrades on the Firestone Tire and Rubber plantation to change the course of history, to make a clean break from modern-day slavery and its peculiar 21st century manifestations. We owe it to ourselves.

Visit www.stopfirestone.org for more information on the Stop Firestone Campaign.

Listen to Robtel Neajai Pailey's interview with Liberian Minister of Labour Kofi Woods and activist Ezekiel Pajibo about the role of Firestone in Liberia at http://www.pambazuka.org/en/broadcasts/index. php

# TRADE, JUSTICE AND
# THE CASE FOR REPARATIONS

**M.P. GIYOSE**

February 2006

Are claims for slavery reparations of US$777 trillion, as made by a 1999 African World Reparations truth commission in Accra, realistic? How does one begin to conceptualise claims for reparations in a broader historical and social context when it comes to centuries of exploitation? M. P. Giyose from Jubilee South Africa makes the case for understanding reparations as a transformation of the way the world functions, ultimately serving to restore and sustain human civilisation.

When a victorious Roman army returned from its conquests, both before and after republican times, it entered the city of Rome in a triumphal march. Of course the procession was bedecked with all manner of loot. Some of the best treasures forcibly taken from vanquished peoples were entered into the Roman treasury as part of the spoils of war. The conquering imperial armies of England, France and Germany in the 18th and 19th centuries followed the old Roman tradition. This kind of 'revenue' has to be distinguished from what in this discussion we call reparations. By the 19th century, European war makers had long refined the custom of a reparations levy. A nation defeated in war was a nation to be doubly punished. When it came to sign the peace treaty, the vanquished nation was given a huge bill, or levy, which it had to pay the victorious party. This was not seen as a tribute, but rather was meant as compensation for the 'losses' or 'the expenditure of war' suffered by the victorious nation. It was, of course, a purely retributive measure, oppressive in every sense. And the defeated nations always understood it to be a form of vengeance.

We need to disclaim altogether any connection between what we are discussing and this kind of payment. The nearest parallel to the notion of reparations is that of damages. Put succinctly, in legal practice the aim of damages is to restore the injured party to the position they would have been in if they had not suffered injury. And whilst this is possible in legal practice, and measurements can come close to scientific exactness, the process is a lot more complex in the arena of political economy. Damages carried out through history are highly rapacious at the point of commission. They carry with them extensive loss of life as well as incalculable material harm. They also carry a historical legacy that puts a nation back by scores of years.

If we understand reparations to be a broad genus, we will also accept that they have a number of species. It is difficult to define reparations, both their general features as well as their specifics, because of the historical and social content of the entire process. We will therefore have to satisfy ourselves with a purely descriptive account of reparations and proceed to our analysis of both the general and specific. Overall, the aim here will be to chart out an economic future for the countries of the South, through a global economic model that is designed to mitigate the woeful history of conquest, economic plunder and financial pillage.

## Global reparations – are they possible?

Let us begin by delineating the entire historical and social process for which reparations are now being determined. From a purely European point of view, capitalism first begins to flex its muscles in the course of the crusades, thus securing a passage for exchanges in goods through Asia Minor to the Indian sub-continent and China. This was reinforced later through the passage around the African continent. Simultaneously, other tentacles spread far and wide into the Atlantic and Caribbean and later to the Pacific islands. The ancient Italian city states of Venice, Florence, Genoa, etc, were thus able to make a rapid transition through feudalism to a capitalist base. The slave trade is one of those reinforcing factors that integrated an African economy, which was at the same time being held back, with the Caribbean islands and the Americas. The road was now open for a transfer of wealth and power from the bankers of the Mediterranean and the Iberian peninsula to the merchant classes in England, Holland and France.

Second, by this time the question of foreign conquest with concomitant ecological brigandage was a settled issue. Third, from quite early on, 20th-century foreign acquisitions took on a financial and industrial colouration. And it was a perfection of this process that took matters a stage further towards the end of the 20th century. The age of globalisation has been the age of subjugation through the sheer power of money.

Each of these four stages of capitalist development has put to the sword not just the liberties of other nations; they have been crucial to the expropriation of their wealth. At each stage the bonds of enslavement have taken on a variety of means, namely: the ecology, labour, trade, debt and investment. Throughout this history, the true indebtedness of Northern societies has stood in direct proportion to the changes in these means.

The questions we have to pose at this stage are: How can the North discharge the settlement of so monumental a debt to Southern societies? Is such a discharge practicable? The questions have to be posed regardless of the lies and mendacious promises given by ruling classes such as those in the USA, in their so-called restorative programmes of upliftment for the slaves whom they took out of the plantation economy of the South. Can the North truly work out a programme of reparations for the South in the emerging economy of our times?

Let us illustrate these questions by offering two examples of claims by representative groups of people from the economic South. In 1999 a truth commission deliberating under the aegis of African World Reparations in Accra demanded reparations of US$777 trillion from Northern nations in compensation for the slave trade, to be paid over five years. Immediately, questions arise: Who exactly is liable for this bill? What are the direct particulars of the offence? To whom are the debtors liable? Has it been possible to establish the actual number of slaves that were extracted out of Africa; the actual number that died in the Middle Passage; the actual number that were landed in America; the actual societies from which the slaves were drawn in Africa? Are these numbers 100 million, or 10 million, or another number in between? Has there been a determination made of exact losses in labour hours from any particular nations or groups of nations in Africa? Or is the quantum of this claim a shot in the dark?

These problems are clearly articulated in the second example to be cited. In a remarkable document submitted to the nations which had 'discovered' a discovery which had been made 40,000 years before, the Native American Chief Guaicaipuro Cuautemoc makes a deposition that is full of scorn, sarcasm, wit and intelligence. At its climax he declares: 'On this basis, and applying the European formula of compound interest, we inform our "discoverers" that they only owe us, as a first payment against

*Reparations can therefore be understood to be a means by which social life in the nations as we know them today can be reformed. In that way they could be seen as an agent for creating 'a better life' for impoverished sections of humanity.*

the debt, a mass of 185,000 kilos of gold and 16 million kilos of sliver, both raised to the power of 300. This equals a figure that would need over 300 digits to put it down on paper and whose weight fully exceeds that of the planet Earth. What huge piles of gold and silver! How much would they weigh when calculated in Blood?'

This is a masterful performance. It refers to one small claim covering a short period of time in historical plunder in a particular location in America: 1503 to 1660. Taken on a world scale, the claims of the countries of the South are literally both astronomical and immeasurable.

On this basis it is perhaps not too difficult to conclude that current Northern societies do not possess the capacity, in spite of their incredible wealth, to repay the debt that they owe the South. Under the punitive reparations of European powers in the 19th century, the combined capacities of all Northern societies would not be able to satisfy a pound-by-pound repayment of all that they owe the South. This is not only a measure of the gargantuan proportions of the Northern debt; it is an indicator of the unimaginable degree of conspicuous consumption among Northern societies in the last 600 years. Clearly, a rational method has to be designed and adopted so that the scales of history can be re-weighted in a manner that would enable the sustained survival of human civilisation in terms of obligations admitted by all sides in today's world.

## Immediate practical proposals

The question of reparations is therefore definitely beyond dispute. What concerns us now as an immediate practical measure is the vehicle we use for negotiating the reparations question. As this needs to be seen from the point of view of the whole world economy, it can only be dealt with in terms of a systemic solution.

Policy-makers have looked at various forms of reparations during our time. Currently, the most vocal intellectual from the nationalist tendency in Africa is President Thabo Mbeki of South Africa. Speaking at the World Economic Forum at Davos in 2001, Mbeki pooh-poohed the very idea of linking economic development in Africa to reparations. The key thing is that there is a Thabo Mbeki in the heartbeat of every other leader in the countries of the South – with one or two exceptions. How can that crop of people then become our agents for a reparations programme, whatever its character may be? That is why we have to fall back for the development of strategy and the discharging of tasks on dynamic political movements operating both in the South and elsewhere.

Sometimes reparations work occurs as piecemeal measures in favour of restorative justice. Some of these may be life and death struggles fought by rural people for land redistribution. At other times conflicts may be joined which are based on some aspects of the debt question. Important examples of this are the struggles over odious debt. These are particularly germane in Southern countries where the debt may have been incurred by dictator regimes, or, at the very least, where there might be a continuing legacy from colonial rape that has compelled successor democratic governments to plunge into debt. Restorative justice could also be used to extend human rights in law. Politically, all these efforts need to be given support especially if they happen as part of a programme.

The ideas now on offer to advance a systemic reparations programme are premised on the integrative forces in the current world situation. That situation consists of three parts. We are presented with a single world political system. This under-girds one economic system that exists on the basis of, and in turn should feed, one ecological system. The three parts make one total world system. It is no longer possible therefore, for us to offer any solutions to the problems of the nations of the South, if these are segregated and can only be expressed through division. A cardinal tenet of an integrated world consists in an understanding that separation, and separate means with 'their own' institutions, can only lead to inequality.

Given these circumstances, measures working in favour of reparations can only be based on the building and sustaining of one world economy – not several pieces thereof. Egalitarian features within the building of the nation will emerge at their very best when they work in conformity with other expressions of the same principle on a world scale. We therefore come to the conclusion that the reorganisation of the world has to occur on the basis of new social foundations – the foundations of a post-capitalist society. This is a society where the forces of equality are universal; they have become the very life force of economics, of ecology and of politics.

## Conclusion

Reparations can therefore be understood to be a means by which social life in the nations as we know them today can be reformed. In that way they could be seen as an agent for creating 'a better life' for impoverished sections of humanity. The need for reparations of this kind is most urgently felt in the countries of the South. However, in the longer view of human history, reparations cannot be viewed as purely ameliorative measures even if they are seen in terms of restorative justice. There is an inbuilt system of 'diminishing returns' in this method of sustaining reparations. In the longer view of historical development, reparations should be seen as an agent for restoring and sustaining human civilisation. And in this way they cannot be a purely national issue. They are an international phenomenon encompassing the combined fortunes of all humankind and all the fauna and flora that keep pace with us in our natural domain.

Women and trade

# WHAT DO WOMEN WANT?

**PAMBAZUKA NEWS STAFF**

September 2006

## What is the role of women in world trade?

Compared to 50 years ago, women represent an increasingly higher proportion of the world's labour force, with many studies placing the number at over 50 per cent. However, this does not include women who work in the informal sector or the unpaid domestic activities of women. On a broader level, women's access to healthcare and education, for example, are profoundly influenced by national economic policy – meaning that if international economic best practice does not take into account gender issues, then women are disadvantaged.

## How does trade have an impact on women's rights?

Trade liberalisation, which refers to the untaxed flow of goods and services between countries, has had positive and negative effects. Increasingly, the negative impacts of trade liberalisation has made trade a central feature of advocacy work by gender activists. Women have gained jobs in the manufacturing sectors, but these jobs may not lead to positive social outcomes as women often work longer hours and are paid low wages. The opening of markets and the influx of cheaper goods have in some cases destroyed livelihoods, and it is women who have borne the brunt of these changes.

## Have women's rights been considered in international trade bodies?

The World Trade Organisation, an international, rules-based and member-driven organisation which oversees a large number of agreements defining the 'rules of trade' between its member states, has long been criticised for not including the voices of women, preferring to view trade as gender neutral. Moreover, its main decision-making bodies are male dominated. To this extent, nothing has been done to take into account or lessen the negative impact of trade liberalisation on women's rights. Despite increasingly loud voices, the WTO refuses to reform itself, has unclear rules about its decision making and does not operate in a transparent manner.

## What is the core of the problem – trade or the global economic system in which we conduct trade?

There is nothing wrong with trade per se; in fact the cornerstone of human society is based on trade. To human beings, trade is a tool for survival. However, a problem arises when one group of people uses trade to exploit and oppress another group of people. From a feminist standpoint, this normally happens in a patriarchal society. A patriarchal society is a society based on the belief that women are inferior to men. The global economic system is shaped and influenced by patriarchal logic. Indirectly and directly, the global economic system cultivates and encourages misogynist attitudes among traders, who nine times out of ten tend to be men.

## What is the alternative?

Or, as patriarchal society puts the question: What do women want?

Women want to be treated with dignity and respect. Lots of feminists have said this before, but women want an end to sex discrimination by job definition and sex-role stereotyping in the media. Like any 'normally' functioning group of people on the planet, women want equity and self-management. Women want a flourishing economy that accomplishes central economic functions without exploiting women, people of colour and the environment. Most importantly, women want an economy that meets people's needs and develops their potential, to paraphrase Michael Albert.

## What is the solution to these problems?

Most governments are already signatories to a host of international agreements committing them to gender equality. These include the UN's Beijing Platform for Action, which requires that governments correct imbalances that any policy, including economic policy, might create.

Economic policies are often fostered on countries by international financial institutions and donors. Officially, consultation on the implementation of these policies does take place, but in reality economic policy should be formulated through a democratic process that takes into account the voices of local people and considers the existing power relations within society.

# WORLD TRADE LIBERALISATION IN AFRICA – WHY WOMEN ARE MOST AFFECTED BY POVERTY

### CHEIKH TIDIANE DIÈYE

September 2006

Africa has faced ten years of unfettered liberalisation that, argues Cheikh Tidiane Dièye, has left the continent on its knees. Women, more than any other group, suffer the weight of the constraints of poverty largely brought about by the world trade system. It is women that must play a crucial role in winning the struggle for a better trading system.

Even though over the last 20 years many African nations have adopted sometimes draconian economic reforms, the benefits of trade liberalisation that were promised have not materialised. On the other hand, developed nations have enjoyed 70 per cent of the wealth generated by trade liberalisation. In some respects, world trade regulations, defined for the most part by industrialised countries during the Uruguay round agreements between 1986 and 1994, have only increased Africa's economic problems.

Before an 'ambiguous consensus'[1] was reached at Doha, at the heart of the multilateral World Trade Organisation (WTO) negotiations, the 'battle of Seattle' or 'Seattle showdown'[2] revealed to the world the growing dissatisfaction of developing countries over the WTO, whose way of working did not appear to respond to their profound desire for economic progress and development.

With the support of strong groups of NGOs, they then put into practice their power to block negotiations by refusing to submit to a potential consensus. With this action – of a kind that was previously unheard of – developing countries, and particularly those in Africa, managed to draw the attention of the international community and the representatives of multilateral institutions to the stark consequences of inequitable globalisation. These consequences have seen hundreds of millions of human beings reduced to near total destitution and the almost irreversible destruction of the environment.

This is why in Seattle, while the United Nations and Europe were seeking to enter into a 'millennium round' of large-scale negotiations concerning new and complex issues, particularly in relation to investment policy, competition, electronic commerce and standards in the areas of labour rights and the environment, a large number of African countries were advocating a 'development round'. Such a round would allow interlocutors to discuss the implementation of regulations from the Uruguay round which directly concern developing countries and to urge industrialised countries to honour their commitments. In this way, these nations hoped finally to succeed in opening developed countries' markets to their exports, eliminating other structural imbalances that were unfavourable to developing nations, removing tariff, non-tariff and technical barriers imposed on the exports of less developed countries, and developing and making official WTO technical aid and capacity building programmes.

From this perspective, the group of African countries proposed to renew and apply the 'special and preferential' measures from the Uruguay agreements, which aimed to facilitate the integration of developing countries into the world trading system.

After Seattle failed, the fourth WTO ministerial conference was held in November 2001 at Doha, Qatar, and the members had a common desire to correct the malfunctioning of the multilateral trading system. The developed countries made a number of promises. Among these were promises to reduce or remove the subsidies causing imbalances in global markets, to remove the obstacles which were blocking develop-

*the 'battle of Seattle' revealed to the world the growing dissatisfaction of developing countries over the WTO, whose way of working did not appear to respond to their profound desire for economic progress and development*

ing countries' products entering their markets, to recognise and make effective special and differential treatment, to facilitate poor countries' access to essential drugs and to create the conditions necessary for the greater participation of these nations in trade negotiations through technical aid and capacity building.

On the other hand, the dogged will of the developed countries to defend the interests of some of their privileged citizens and their multinationals immediately took priority over ethical considerations and concerns for the survival of African populations: access to essential drugs for millions of sick Africans is still being blocked due to market interests; millions of farmers sink into poverty each day as a result of the North's illegal subsidies;[3] and the pressure to increase the liberalisation of basic social services such as water, education, energy and healthcare is about to destroy what remains of African economies.

One of the most tangible characteristics of African poverty is its 'femininity'. Statistics show that African women, more so than any other category, suffer the damaging effects of poverty and all the constraints brought about by the current structure of global economic and trade relations. In healthcare as well as in education, access to land and economic resources, African women have remained well below world averages.

In such a context, it is not difficult to establish a link between the situation of women in Africa and the world trade system, which, even if it is not the only explanatory factor, is at the very least an important factor. The financial collapse of agriculture and African industries, caused by the combined effect of liberal policies imposed by international financial institutions and WTO rules, affects both rural and urban women, as it subjects them to chronic food insecurity, begging and the dangers of the informal economy in African towns and cities.

## Greater liberalisation does not give rise to human development

Many studies have tried to establish a correlation between the level of openness to trade and increased economic growth and human development. However, there is no proof that the liberalisation of exchanges leads automatically to economic growth and human development. In a study[4] looking at the relationship between trade and sustainable human development, the UNDP drew an interesting comparison between two countries, in relation to their level of openness to world trade, to demonstrate such an assertion. These countries are Vietnam and Haiti.

Since the beginning of the 1980s, Vietnam has undertaken a progressive approach to reform. It is not a member country of the WTO. It has organised world trade at the level of the state, has maintained a monopoly over imports, and has preserved quan-

---

*the pressure to increase the liberalisation*
*of basic social services such as water, education,*
*energy and healthcare is about to destroy*
*what remains of African economies*

---

titative restrictions and high customs duties (30 to 50 per cent) on imports of agricultural and industrial products. However, despite these measures being contrary to the 'formulas' often advocated by the proponents of neoliberal doctrines, Vietnam has had spectacular success by achieving a growth rate higher than 8 per cent per annum since the mid-1980s, which has earned the country a 12 per cent increase in trade, a considerably reduced level of poverty, including in rural areas and among vulnerable groups (women and young people), and has attracted high levels of foreign direct investment.

Haiti, on the other hand, has embarked on an ambitious road to liberalisation and total openness since 1994/95. The country has brought its customs tariffs down to a maximum of 15 per cent and has removed all quantitative restrictions. Despite all this, Haiti's economy has not evolved. Social indicators have even deteriorated and poverty has, in places, reached worrying levels. Although a member of the WTO, Haiti is one of the most marginal countries in terms of integration into world trade.

Looking at Africa, an analysis of the evolution of world trade over the last 20 years shows that the continent has unfortunately not profited from the benefits[5] that were granted. Despite all the agreements and preferential schemes, Africa's share of world trade has dropped significantly from 6 per cent in 1980 to 2 per cent in 2004. In effect, since 1980, African exports have increased at the average annual rate of 1.5 per cent, whereas for the world as whole this increased by 5.8 per cent per year.

The social consequences of such economic decline no longer need to be explained. In sub-Saharan Africa, women in certain areas produce up to 80 per cent of basic food products and therefore play a decisive role in food security for both the family and the nation. And in areas where cash crops predominate, reduced earnings resulting from reduced tariff protections and the large-scale entry of imported goods into national markets has exacerbated the vulnerability of women. They have no option other than to add to the swelling populations of shanty towns to work in informal jobs and small trade in order to survive.

In the industrial sector, WTO agreements on rules for market access for non-agricultural goods have imposed drastic cuts in customs duties, which were the only instrument for protecting African industries. This subjects a growing, and consequently vulnerable, African industry to direct confrontation with big corporations from the

*It is remarkable that the mediocre results achieved for African nations after ten years of liberalisation under the aegis of the WTO has not led developed countries to reassess their positions and objectives.*

developed countries, which has quickly worked to the advantage of the latter. The most instructive example today is the African textile industry, in which countries with a definite relative advantage were obliged to cut hundreds of thousands of jobs even before the agreement on quotas was reached in December 2004. And since 2005, China's powerful entry into the world textile market has heightened the pressure in this sector. Nigeria, Tunisia, Morocco, Ghana, Senegal and other countries are today experiencing the full force of the crisis in this industry, which has a high employment capacity, including for women.

Even if the liberalisation of the textile industry has increased and diversified the supply of goods in African markets, where prices have also tended to drop, such an outcome cannot compensate for the long-term losses that the de-industrialisation of Africa will bring about. This de-industrialisation has only increased the informalisation of the economy by developing trade around goods produced elsewhere.

## The WTO ten years on: economic opportunities or fresh risks?

The ten years of liberalisation under the aegis of the WTO needs to be assessed. Disregarding doctrine and squabbles between different schools of thought, it has been widely accepted that for African countries, trade liberalisation has not produced the results hoped for.

Even if one has to admit that it is often difficult to measure the real impact of WTO rules on women in Africa, specific studies, of which there is a real shortage in this area, have concluded that this impact is most worrying when compared with the overall assessment of WTO rules on African populations.

Studies conducted into the liberalisation of the water sector in many African countries have shown that it is mainly women who carry the burden of the fresh constraints brought about by the privatisation of these strategic sectors. In the field of work, liberalisation has certainly increased the opportunities available to women in certain countries, but this usually takes place in very poor conditions and often pays much less.

It is remarkable that the mediocre results achieved for African nations after ten years of liberalisation under the aegis of the WTO has not led developed countries to reassess their positions and objectives. If the negotiations have today become bogged down in differences of opinion such that they have been indefinitely 'suspended' by the director of the WTO, this is not because the organisation is trying to take better account of the interests of developing nations, and Africans in particular. The present crisis is mainly down to the battle between the United States and the European Union on the one side, and the G20[6] on the other. The battle is over the issue of parallelism[7] of forms. The developed countries are calling for the developing countries to impose drastic cuts in customs duties on industrial goods and to commit to the liberalisation of the trade in services, whereas the developing countries are calling for the other nations to reduce their agricultural subsidies.

Given the present crisis and the gloomy prospects at the WTO, the logical conclusion of an evaluation of its 10 years of action should be 'mission unaccomplished'.

The question to ask now is what should be the alternative to the WTO? What would be the consequences of a long-term crisis at the WTO for African people, and women in particular?

It is extremely tempting to respond in a simplistic way by saying that the failure of negotiations at the WTO could only be to the advantage of African countries due to the unfairness of the current rules. However, if one looks at the power relations at the WTO and in the system of world governance, this stance is not backed up by clear analysis. The failure of trade negotiations would allow the status quo to gain acceptance once and for all, and would reinforce current trade relations, which are mostly to the detriment of African nations.

Therefore, we must relaunch multilateral negotiations and fight, so that the principle of special and differential treatment for African nations is put in place, made effective and made obligatory, in accordance with the Doha mandate, in all areas of the negotiations.

Even if the negotiations have still not really advanced the cause of Africa, they at least allow African populations to take an interest in them, place more popular pressure on governments and negotiators, provide a platform for African states and civil society organisations (NGOs, producer organisations, trade unions, women's organisations, etc) to denounce current trade rules and schemes, and reduce the pressure from governments in the North and multilateral institutions who advocate liberalisation in the interests of the rich.

## Conclusion

The way in which trade is governed in today's world leads to necessarily unfair results. But could it be otherwise in a game whose players are not equal?

Whilst the rules that have been set do not allow African nations to develop the means to compensate those who have been damaged by international trade, developed nations have implemented mechanisms to protect themselves from the dangers brought about by liberalisation.

In such a context, the Doha development agenda could only really achieve its goal of creating a framework for development if it allowed the creation of an international environment that guarantees African countries enough flexibility to implement national standards and policies. This would have the effect of helping these nations protect their populations, markets and institutions from the effects of the market.

Such an approach calls upon African leaders to act responsibly. If it is understood that the system governing world trade should take greater account of the opinions of vulnerable populations, we also need to recognise that this task must first be carried out at the national level. Greater participation of various types of stakeholders, including politicians, NGOs, producer organisations, women, consumers, the private sector, etc, in the development of trade policy is without doubt a pre-requisite for making national interests known at WTO negotiations. From the perspective of gender,[8] however, even though efforts have been made for years, there remains a serious shortfall that is holding back African negotiation strategies.

This is a shortened version of the original French article, which was translated by Timothy Cleary.

**Notes**

1 See *Passerelles* 3(2), November 2001–January 2002.

2 From a book by Maude Barlow and Tony Clarke (*Global Showdown: How the New Activists are Fighting Global Corporate Rule*, 2002), recounting the demonstrations of global citizens' movements which prevented the launch of the WTO's millenium round.

3 Interesting studies conducted by NGOs such as Enda Third World, Oxfam and the International Centre for Trade and Sustainable Development (ICSTD) have shown the disastrous impact of American subsidies on the African cotton trade. On this, read the 'White paper on cotton', Enda Diapol, 2005.

4 UNDP (2003) *Making Global Trade Work for People*, UNDP.

5 Among these relative benefits, one can cite in particular the non-reciprocal trade preferences between the EU and the ACP which characterised the Lomé Convention, the flexibility offered to less developed countries at the WTO and, more generally, to the generalised system of preferences.

6 The G20 is a large group of negotiators based around the big developing countries which export agricultural goods, such as India, Brazil, Argentina, China and South Africa. The group emerged just before the Cancun conference in 2003 and is fighting against subsidies in the North.

7 This is a concept defended by the EU in particular in its commitments. Each group stands firm and asks the other groups to make the first commitments.

8 Few of the African delegations at the WTO ministerial conference in Hong Kong included women.

# TRADE, GENDER AND THE SEARCH
# FOR ALTERNATIVES – TRADE LIBERALISATION
# AND SOCIAL DEVELOPMENT

### JENNIFER CHIRIGA

February 2006

It is women who bear the brunt of the effects of trade liberalisation on social development through a lack of access to basic social services. But, writes Jennifer Chiriga from the Alternative Information and Development Centre, one of the major impacts of trade on women is how the capitalist ethic plays into building masculinity while at the same time downplaying the role of women in society. Alternatives are in the offing, she argues.

The defining trends of current trade and economic relations across the globe and the process through which current international economic relations are played out, and markets for products and services are increasingly being defined, all fall under the rubric of globalisation.

International trade expansion has in the last few decades been manifesting a profound transformation, with the emergence of integration of economic activity, including elimination of restrictions on the free movement across borders of capital, goods, resources, technology and services. All regions of the world are coming closer together through intensified trade, investment, financial transactions, and information technology. Unfortunately the global expansion has not affected developing regions evenly, and Africa continues to lag behind.

The main feature of globalisation is a surge in the power of global capital and reorganising of global production through multinational corporations that wield tremendous influence over economies. Globalisation has been quite aptly cited as 'largely the game of the powerful ... the strong do what they will, and the weak must surrender what they cannot protect'.[1]

Other defining characteristics of globalisation are a more integrated global economy with interdependencies among nations, the benefits of which accrue to developed economies; a decline in investment in production, with companies moving more towards speculative investment, which brings faster and higher profits; a diminishing public sector, with the state becoming more business-oriented through privatisation of state enter-prises; and the phenomenal power of multinational corporations that have the clout to drive global trade and influence governments, as seen by the power of the World Bank (WB), International Monetary Fund (IMF) and World Trade Organisation (WTO).

The WTO is not just about trade: it is about power and the control of resources. Developed countries shape and control the trade regimes that affect developing coun-tries and that lead to de-industrialisation, job losses and the worsening of poverty. This is evidenced by the experience of developing countries that are undergoing IMF/WB enforced structural adjustment programmes, who have been forced to liberalise their external trade, and have subsequently suffered destruction of local industries leading to massive retrenchments.

In spite of the conventional understanding about the creation of an 'open' global free trade system, there is very limited 'free trade', particularly for African countries.

---

*one of the key considerations is that the mobilisation of strong social movements and organisations can provide the pressure and impetus that will eventually cause a shift in the global balance of power*

---

The relevance of the WTO in the world system is that it is seen as the central institu-tion in a centralised global economy. This has major relevance for African countries as they grapple with huge development challenges. The external orientation of African countries has led to the opening up of global markets, resulting in the flooding in of imports and the domination of foreign products, such as agricultural produce and textiles. This has led to massive loss of jobs in rural and urban sectors, threats to food security and the abandonment of the social development project. The effects of trade liberalisation on social development is evidenced by the lack of access to basic social services, with women bearing the greater burden.

## Gender and trade

One of the major factors in gender inequality relates to how negative perceptions mould gender differences and how the capitalist ethic plays into building masculinity while at the same time playing down the role that women play in society, where they occupy the role of secondary earners. Gender is a key determinant of vulnerability to poverty. And women, due to their disadvantaged position in the labour market, hold lower paid jobs that require lower levels of skills.

Although gender analysts have for a long time emphasised the negative impacts of trade liberalisation, the link between gender and trade has been tenuous, largely because gender considerations have been perceived as irrelevant; they are given no place at the negotiating table where trade issues are discussed. Looked at through a gender prism, trade policies have grave implications for the development and well-being of women because of their impact on employment, poverty and the social burden carried by women. Although women are an important and significant constituency, there is no evidence of a gender perspective when trade policy is being formulated in the WTO.

A study on policy links between gender and trade[2] emerged with a number of 'reality points' that link gender and trade, and make a case for the importance of putting gender analysis at the centre of trade policy.

## Changes in social service delivery affect women to a greater extent

Trade policies and trade liberalisation can affect the ability of governments to finance social sector expenditure. The observation is that any revenue shortfalls leading to a reduction in government expenditure affects social service delivery, and the burden is shifted to the households and women. The study states that in 1993 women contributed over US$11 trillion worth of household work to the world economy, and that trade policy should therefore not ignore women's unwaged work in social reproduction. Gender planning should be built into the design of trade policies. A key point is that social development should be the bedrock of trade policy since women's traditional roles do not make it easy for them to access opportunities to engage in international trade.

## Entrenched gender inequalities in the labour market are unfavourable to women

The labour market tends to be segmented on gender lines with inequalities in income, career advancement and conditions of work. Traditionally, expansion of trade is based on access to low-wage labour, which is mainly female labour. Liberalisation of trade and the surge of foreign capital and transnational corporations maintain competitiveness through minimising the costs of production, especially labour costs. While one can generalise the negative effects on the labour market, for women the impact is higher – they have lower wages and less bargaining power because unions tend to be dominated by a male leadership. The danger of trade liberalisation bringing greater hardship for women is very real – because sub-contracting and flexible work allows corporations to avoid direct financial responsibility for workers.

## Women have less access to economic resources: credit, skills and technical assistance

Institutionalised discrimination affects women's access to land and credit from financial institutions, and therefore impacts in a very fundamental way on their role in the economy. When trade barriers are reduced and an infusion of cheaper imports come into the market, women may lose out especially when quality control becomes an issue and introduces lack of competitiveness.

---

*The WTO is not just about trade; it is about power and the control of resources. Developed countries shape and control the trade regimes that affect developing countries and that lead to de-industrialisation, job losses and the worsening of poverty.*

---

One of the major gaps is that while WTO rules encompass all levels of economic development, there is no gender analysis that assesses these rules in a structured way. While there is a ready source of scientific research documenting the realities of women's lives and how the economy impacts on them, the conceptual and policy links between gender and trade have to be given more attention. Further analysis of the link between gender and trade policy should look at the following questions:

- Are trade policies geared towards the elimination of poverty and gender inequality?
- Do trade rules prevent government and private businesses from formulating gender-sensitive policies?
- Are trade policies based on competition that ignores reproductive tasks? In other words, do they reinforce the masculine model of superiority?

Even as we grapple with the specific gender dimensions, trade policy should not be approached in isolation of macro-level economic policy. In this context, the discussion of alternatives raises very broad issues.

## Alternative strategies for development

Change is possible through a break from the mainstream model of dominant global capital. The emergence of national, regional and international forums such as the Africa Social Forum (ASF) and the World Social Forum (WSF) is a sign that there is an increas-

## Kenya: women workers turn to flower power

### June 2006

Kenya is covered by numerous trade agreements, including the African Growth and Opportunity Act (AGOA), the African, Caribbean and Pacific – European Union (ACP–EU) Trade Agreement and the Common Market of Eastern and Southern Africa (COMESA). According to the Export Processing Zones Authority of Kenya, all these open the region up to trade and allow for preferential treatment, including duty and quota free benefits and regional free trade. In addition to these trade agreements, Kenya has received financial assistance from the World Bank and USAID to get its agricultural industries off the ground, reports the International Labour Rights Fund.

The agricultural sector falls under all of these trade agreements and accounts for almost a quarter of Kenya's GDP. Almost 75 per cent of the population relies on agriculture, whether directly or indirectly, and the flower industry employs at least 50,000 Kenyans directly and another 70,000 in related industries. According to the Export Processing Zones Authority of Kenya, cut flowers dominate the horticulture exports, and this crop has overtaken both coffee and tourism as a source of foreign exchange. The EU currently receives the largest portion of Kenya's cut flowers, but the country's flowers end up as far as Asia, Australia and the US.

While Kenya's government benefits economically from this industry, critics argue that people, and women especially, are suffering as a result of lax laws, environmental hazards, dangerous working conditions and harmful power dynamics. According to the report by the International Labour Rights Fund, over half of Kenyan flower workers are employed only as 'casuals', and as such, they do not receive benefits, cannot join unions and have no job security. Further, the Kenya Human Rights Commission reveals that workers are often forced to do unpaid overtime, working as long as 12 hours a day, with few breaks. Many employees have been exposed to dangerous toxins from the fertilisers and pesticides that are used on the crops, which often lead to skin irritations, problems with sight and many more unknown effects, according to an article entitled 'Cut flower industry accused of human rights abuse'.

As a result of these human rights violations, local groups are letting the industry know that the working conditions they are forced into are not acceptable. With the help of Women Working Worldwide, the Kenya Women Workers Organisation has highlighted the plight of flower workers. They undertake various projects, including non-violent campaigns for workers' rights, lobbying and advocacy, community development projects, capacity building and the encouragement of women's participation in decision-making processes. Through their work they raise awareness and offer support to women exploited in Kenya's flower industry.

**Sources**

*Export Processing Zones Authority of Kenya <http://www.epzakenya.com/aboutkenya.php?cat=4&sub=15>*

*International Labour Rights Fund (ILRF) (2003) 'Codes of conduct in the cut-flower industry', ILRF Working Paper <http://www.labor-rights.org/projects/women/Flower_Paper_0903/flower_paper_countries.htm>*

*Kenya Women Workers Organisation <http://www.kewwo.org>*

*Cathy Majtenyi (2002) 'Cut flower industry accused of human rights abuse' <http://www.newsfromafrica.org/newsfromafrica/articles/art_882.html>*

ing trend for organisations and social movements which mobilise to reflect and exchange ideas on alternative visions and actions. The WSF was conceived as a response to the growing struggle against neoliberalism and as an alternative to the World Economic Forum where business leaders from all over the world get together to discuss the economic state of the world. The WSF is an arena for debate, as well as an opportunity for social movements and activists from the North and South to meet and exchange ideas.

There is already a powerful discourse, which is, however, being undermined by the concentration of wealth and the antidemocratic strength of powerful global corporations. Nevertheless, the emergence of regionalism as an alternative is gaining ground as a possible solution to the dislocation of Africa's economic potential.

The questions to pose in any deliberations on alternatives are:

- How can we engender the political will necessary for the regional project?
- How can we harness the geopolitical concept of regionalism to engage and challenge the globalised system on a stronger footing?
- How can Africa turn regional integration and cooperation groupings into real frameworks for alternative models of development?

Africa already has some examples of a unique regional integration model that has roots in pan-African solidarity. There is potential for strengthened regional blocs to encompass the development needs of emerging economies. Regional integration has the potential to break the leverage that industrial countries have over Africa, where governments need to realise that engaging the local with the regional and continental is the future in terms of economic development.

In response to the questions raised above, one of the key considerations is that mobilisation of strong social movements and organisations can provide the pressure and impetus that will eventually cause a shift in the global balance of power. Social movements should be the foundation of a people-based process that promotes developmental regionalism, centred on human rights, women's rights and social justice. Commitment should be to a unified region in which local and community-based development is the primary underpinning of national and regional development programmes.

Through strategic interdependencies we need to redirect trade to domestic and regional spaces, increase manufacturing and production and add value to our primary products. In addition, the liberalisation and privatisation policies should be replaced and we should create trade and development cooperation agreements that reflect the realities and needs of the people, and that are not predetermined or constricted by compliance with WTO terms and conditionalities.

Cooperative development would ensure, for example, that shared resources such as energy and water could be approached holistically for the benefit of the whole region. But as long as powerful economies like South Africa continue to follow a sub-imperialist agenda, it will be a lost battle. African governments must cooperate, coordinate and combine. As someone said at a workshop recently, 'extroverted economies will get us nowhere'.

**Notes**

1 Tandon cited in P. Vale and S. Maseko (1998) 'South Africa and the African renaissance', *International Affairs* 74(2).

2 Informal Working Group on Gender and Trade (IWGGT) (1998) *Gender and Trade; Some Conceptual and Policy Links*. Geneva: IWGGT.

# WOMEN AND GLOBALISATION –
# THE IMPACT ON THEIR HEALTH

### MOUHAMADOU TIDIANE KASSE

October 2006

Mouhamadou Tidiane Kasse argues that the implementation of neoliberal policies and strategies in Africa, which have culminated in globalisation, resulted in the feminisation of poverty on the continent. 'Liberalisation began by hitting social services. Women were to suffer the most from the effects, because of traditions and their social position.'

Today, two concepts stand together. They work in parallel, but also together, since, inevitably, the two situations they encompass feed off one another. Since the beginning of the 1980s and the implementation of neoliberal policies and strategies in Africa, which have culminated in globalisation, the feminisation of poverty has become an irreversible, downward spiral. Among the consequences of this in the 1990s was that the spread of Aids in Africa began to take on a feminine character.

As poverty becomes more feminine, so Aids takes hold. In the first decade after its appearance, the disease was mainly rife among men, but now its distribution has been reversed to the detriment of women. Of the 25 million people living with HIV in Africa (out of 37.8 million globally), 58 per cent are women. The proportions are the same for the 9,000 people who contract the virus every day in Africa.

The feminisation of poverty and its effects on women's health are preventable. Neoliberal policies began to take control in Africa from the 1980s onwards. The economic and financial recovery plan (EFRP) of the 1970s was followed by structural adjustment programmes (SAPs) in the 1980s, and poverty reduction strategy papers (PRSPs) in the 1990s. The semantic shifts show the successive failures of these policies, which were set up by the World Bank and the International Monetary Fund and locked Africa into an endless spiral of poverty. All these policies have today resulted in globalisation, which has moved the continent's fragility up one level, with disastrous effects. What previously happened merely at a local level, within states, now takes place on a global scale, transcending borders and state sovereignty.

The template for today's tragedy was drawn in the 1980s. Liberalisation began by hitting social services. Women were to suffer the most from the effects, because of traditions and their social position. The decision to make access to education more and more expensive led to girls falling behind. Twenty years later, millions have had to be invested to provide them with an education to make up for the effects of this disaster. At the same time, mortality rates among mothers and children went beyond scandalous and the reduction of these rates is now one of the development goals of the new millennium. These policies are like emptying a barrel just so that it can be refilled. This is serious when human lives are at stake.

## Survival strategies

The findings of a study entitled *Les familles dakaroises face à la crise* (Families in Dakar confronting the crisis) told a worrying story about the years following the implementation of liberal policies:

> It is in fact wage earners in the private sector who are most acutely affected by the crisis of the 1980s. Among men, the unemployed make up 13.7 per cent of industry. In construction, the figure is 14.3 per cent, it is 4.6 per cent in the private service sector and production and 9.1 per cent in business. The agricultural and fishing industries have been hit the hardest by unemployment (18.8 per cent). But the situation is all the more tragic for women, whose level of unemployment is 21.6 per cent in industry, 15.0 per cent in the service sector and production and 19.2 per cent in business. The higher levels of unemployment among women are so acute that many have had to state that they are housewives after looking for work in vain. The figures given for women are therefore low estimates for female unemployment.[1]

The continued process of world trade liberalisation has created a context of economic and social disintegration, with women suffering the most in Africa. In the two-tier societies that are being set up, the effects are piling up at the end of the line. Here, women are the final – and weakest – link. Girls are being deprived of an education, ruining their futures through teenage pregnancy, and wives are experiencing all manner of marital violence (latent or visible, codified or not by society), which is exacerbated by poverty and the absence of life's basic necessities.

The survival strategies women have employed – becoming workers in production or industry – do not stand up to new de-protection laws. Factories close or streamline their staff and imports kill off whole sections of production. Today, female traders in Africa have to go ever further to compete with Asian products that are flooding the markets. As one Senegalese woman put it:

In the 1980s, I used to go to Gambia. When the 1990s came, I had to go as far as Nouakchott and Las Palmas to develop my business. Today, you have to go to Dubai, Taiwan and Hong Kong to compete with the markets that have been established where we are, especially with the Chinese. Investment is more expensive, journeys are longer and difficulties are greater when it comes to reconciling our role as pillars of the family and our economic functions. In the group of women with whom I organise alternate trips and shared purchasing, we spend hundreds of millions of francs on business each year. But because we work informally, because we do not offer the guarantees deemed necessary, the state will not support us and banks will no longer offer us credit.

So, laws do not work in women's favour and the social environment even less so. Natalie Domeisen, of the ITC International Trade Forum, is quoted as saying:

Do women encounter added difficulties when trying to expand their trade through exports because they are women? This is precisely the fundamental question societies should be asking themselves and should be agreeing upon in order to speed up change. For small businesses, access to finances, market information and training is essential. Women who are involved in exports have, however, fewer opportunities to access the support networks that a good number of their male counterparts have. The type of assistance they need is also different. Most businesses belonging to women are part of the service industry, and the main way of developing these businesses is by setting up networks with a view to creating a client base.

## Life and health

The great majority of women, however, are far from these concerns of market dominance. Instead, daily concerns revolve around health and survival strategies. One major concern today is that millions of women do not have access to the healthcare during pregnancy and childbirth that could save their lives. For example, only 53 per cent of births in developing countries take place with the assistance of a qualified person (a doctor, midwife or nurse). With the poor nutritional condition of women before pregnancy, healthcare that is inadequate, inaccessible or too expensive, not to mention the lack of hygiene and care during labour, there has been a huge increase in dangerous pregnancies.

Beyond the failures of national policies, globalisation has turned healthcare into a market area, and drugs into a market good. The debate and conflict between countries in the South and the North in relation to the Agreements on Intellectual Property Rights (TRIPS), under the framework of the World Trade Organisation (WTO), have been instructive. Supported by the patents they hold, drug multinationals have been opposed to certain products being made in countries in the South, where local industry could do this job in order to reduce prices and improve the health of populations. The issue made the headlines in 2000, when 39 drugs companies started legal proceedings against South Africa for allowing its population access to low-cost drugs, particularly anti-retrovirals. In April 2001, they withdrew their action when African states raised their shields by sticking to safeguards. The agreement on TRIPS requires WTO member governments to ensure, over a period of 20 years, copyright and patent protection for various new products, including pharmaceutical products. Without the consent of the inventor, no one can use, make or sell a particular product during this period. In the meantime, Aids is killing people – and particularly more and more women. The 2005 UNAIDS data for sub-Saharan Africa shows that 58 per cent of infected adults are women.

To end this pandemic and slow down its effects, anti-retroviral treatment required, at one point, 600,000 CFA francs per month (around $1,000; the costs have been reduced since then and the drugs are even free in certain countries thanks to public spending). Yet it would have been possible to produce generic drugs locally, thus reducing costs.

*The issue made the headlines in 2000, when 39 drugs companies started legal proceedings against South Africa for allowing its population access to low-cost drugs*

In India, a pharmaceutical group set the price of anti-retrovirals at $600 (per person, per year) for African governments. However, between the rights of patent holders and the right to life for millions and millions of people, it was necessary to reach a contentious legal decision. Brazil had to face attacks from America for adopting a law that authorised local production of anti-retroviral drugs such as AZT, which helps to prevent transmission from mother to child.

With the mobilisation of countries in the South, ethics took precedence over profit. After threatening South Africa with sanctions at a point when the country was wrestling with American pharmaceutical companies, President Bill Clinton signed a decree to change American intellectual property laws on the distribution of drugs to counter HIV/Aids in sub-Saharan Africa. This decree forbade anyone from lodging a complaint to the WTO in order to block the wishes of sub-Saharan African countries to produce or obtain drugs to fight Aids.

The market logic that is taking hold of healthcare is doing so because this sector is an enormous source of revenue – from drugs, the provision of healthcare, laboratory materials, etc. Even now under the WTO, the precedence of the right to healthcare over patent rights has yet to become a reality. Even if small gains have been made, the United States remains tied to the idea that a wider agreement on property rights could tomorrow be extended to the diseases that generate much higher profits for laboratories.

In effect, even if the debate has focused on diseases like tuberculosis, malaria and Aids, medical research on these three most deadly pandemics comes to less than 5 per cent of the total budget for research at the ten largest pharmaceutical companies in the world. But to make concessions in this domain is seen as a threat to making a tidy profit. A case in point is the sale of drugs that are threatened by the arrival of generic drugs between now and 2007, which is valued at $50 billion – $17.8 billion of which go to the American companies Merck and Pfizer.

This is how some people's billions are the source of other people's misfortune. According to the current logic of globalisation, world trade rules control national policy. We are witnessing the loss of sovereignty and international agreements are directly influencing public policy. In social services such as healthcare and education, finance ministers determine what is invested and what is undertaken according to the standards of international financial markets. The wild logic of economic gain thus takes precedence over the necessities of social well-being.

In Mali, for example, the fight against malaria has at its disposal neither the necessary financial means nor an adequate institutional policy. The national programme is only one of the areas of the prevention division of the National Health Directorate, and has a budget of 1.5 billion CFA francs ($2.9 million) per year. And to take even the smallest actions requires considerable efforts to move things along. Yet, according to the United

---

*The market logic that is taking hold of healthcare is doing so because this sector is an enormous source of revenue – from drugs, the provision of healthcare, laboratory materials, etc.*

---

Nations' 2005 report on the Millennium Development Goals, malaria destroys a million lives each year, mainly women and young children – consequently slowing down economic growth by 1.3 per cent per year. And 90 per cent of these deaths take place in sub-Saharan Africa, where more than 2,000 children are lost to this disease every day. Mali is among those countries where this disease is still endemic, and requires prevention and constant funding.

Since the 1980s, African countries have done nothing but put up with this. But do they have the means to resist? The partial failure of the last WTO ministerial summit in Hong Kong in December 2005, which was supposed to close the Doha round after the Cancun stage in September 2003 (which also failed), was due to the mobilisation of countries in the South against a process that places them in an endless trap. But

*In social services such as healthcare and education, finance ministers determine what is invested and what is undertaken according to the standards of international financial markets. The wild logic of economic gain thus takes precedence over the necessities of social well-being.*

the resistance over cotton, where the reserves of countries in Asia, Latin America and Africa, on top of other issues, are not enough to stop the machine called globalisation. The WTO is but one structural framework to have ended in failure. Meanwhile, the process continues according to its own dynamic, led by multinationals.

Resistance from civil society, through the mobilisation of the anti-globalisation movement, remains a very weak obstacle. This movement has struggled to take root in wider society and the proportion of women in it remains very slight. In the demonstrations of the African Social Forum, the female component is still very marginal. It is less a vehicle for reflecting on resistance and alternatives to globalisation than an appendix to the changes that are being sought. We continue to debate what we put up with (physical violence, mental violence and so on) rather than the solutions and tools available to women.

In the current climate of the feminisation of poverty and the feminisation of disease, the vicious circle is getting larger and affecting more and more women; at the same time it is closing in on them as part of a continued process that is making insecurity more widespread. Page (2000) writes:

The subordination of women in African society, in the face of the HIV/Aids pandemic, is leading to premature deaths and the break-up of millions of families across the whole of the [African] continent. The fact that this in turn is creating a generation of rootless and traumatised children will have grave consequences for the future stability of many countries in Africa. While we concentrate solely on preventing infection and caring for those who are dying, we are neglecting the opportunity to prolong the healthy and productive lives of Africans who are HIV-positive, particularly mothers with children of a young age.

The logic of globalisation does not want this process to end.

111

This article was translated from the original French by Timothy Cleary.

**Notes**

1 P. Antoine, P. Bocquier et al (1995) *Les familles dakaroises face à la crise*. Paris: IFAN–ORSTOM–CEPED.

# WHAT DO WOMEN STAND TO GAIN FROM TRADE?
# – WOMEN IN BUSINESS AND COMMERCE
## SALMA MAOULIDI

September 2006

Trade, trade and more trade: that's the winning formula for a fulfilled life. But what does this mean for women in East Africa? How are their interests reflected in trading activities? Salma Maoulidi investigates.

Trade signifies an assortment of economic activities and transactions. Trade, for many in the global South struggling to improve their economic status, is the new salvation. It is the magic equation to economic prosperity – do more of it and up goes your gross domestic product (GDP), winning you points in economic performance.

But like all prevailing economic formulas there is a catch: for any meaningful economic gains to be registered under the present trade regime, external trading must outweigh internal trading. In practical terms this means economies import more at the expense of local production, the latter becoming more prohibitive and less competitive on account of higher production and transaction costs. Conversely, countries fetch lower returns on exports following the devaluation of local currencies, making then too weak to trade competitively on the world market. Exports also earn less because goods produced locally continue to have the inferior status of 'raw materials' or unprocessed goods and are of a lesser value compared to processed goods.

## Why sex is a factor in the trade equation

In simple terms, this is how the current trade regime functions. Underneath this simplicity, however, lies a complex set of relationships that fundamentally influence the terms and players in trade deals, including women. Universally, the world of business is seen to be off limits to women. Just as dominant religious and cultural ideologies persistently deny women proprietary rights, the business establishment has followed suit, recognising more readily women's role as producers and as consumers, but not as owners and managers of productive enterprise.

Political independence has had minimal impact on the national and global profile of wealth distribution. During colonial times in East Africa, the trading class was composed mainly of Indians and a few Arabs, who owned the local retail and wholesale shops. The main economic activities, however, were controlled by the settler farmer and colonial administration, mostly Europeans. As corporations take over economic activities, trade monopoly is no longer solely defined by race and ethnicity. Thus the local Indian or Arab retailer in East Africa is being replaced by the Chinese retailer or wholesaler while an expert labour force from India and other parts of South East Asia take over industries and the service sector. A few indigenous entrepreneurs claim a stake in local and regional business, but for the most part Africans form the bulk of the unskilled labour force and remain the primary consumers.

The sex composition in the business world has remained unchanged, with women registering little success in penetrating global, regional and local markets. Women in trade and economic bodies are still under-represented. In Tanzania, for example, women are underrepresented in virtually all business chambers. The local bourse has very few women traders as do local industries. Regional trade agreements offer business opportunities beyond national boundaries but are, for the most part, not integrative of the needs of women. Trade frameworks like NEPAD or the East African common markets, while seemingly progressive, are rendered ineffective by constitutional frameworks that preserve national gender inequalities. In many respects, therefore, women remain objects of sale, convenient conduits for furthering materialist aims and gains. They have yet to become the subject of trade regimes and investments.

## The miracle of women-friendly economic programmes

In view of the persistent exclusion of women from economic enterprise and the widespread belief that economic empowerment is critical to raising the status of women, some quarters, either pioneering individuals or development organisations, have tried to redress the imbalance of players in economic enterprise. Many implement programmes aimed at the economic upliftment of women, programmes that vary minimally in approach in that they have micro-lending or microcredit as the basis for women's economic empowerment.

The theory of women and economic upliftment is, however, flawed as it does not see the woman as an independent economic investor or dealer. Indeed, whereas the imperialist business model focuses on accumulation in order to achieve profit maximisation through serious capital injection, prevailing notions of women and entrepreneurship limit women's economic engagement to the micro, the small business happening outside the margins of real business.

Essentially, the very concept of microcredit is restrictive. Other than suggesting that it is insignificant, and therefore of minimal consequence, in so far as volume and risk is concerned, it does not view women as serious accumulators of capital. Rather, the concern is to give women enough to help them and their families survive. Such an outlook has affected how women engage in business, their overwhelming motivation being aiding their families, not making serious money.

Indeed, women plough back most of the earnings and profits from productive activities into their families instead of expanding or diversifying their businesses (a fact a number of agencies have relied on to introduce or intensify microcredit programmes targeting women). Because women's economic activity is mainly concerned with improving household and family welfare it is not perceived as a serious trade venture.

> *prevailing notions of women and entrepreneurship limit*
> *women's economic engagement to the micro, the small*
> *business happening outside the margins of real business*

Perhaps if women did not assume the greater burden of caring for the household, they would dare trade for profit as some younger unattached women do. They would vie to make money for the sake of making money and not just for survival.

The terms of engagement under which most micro-lending schemes operate are also limiting in that they require women to organise in collectives – in fives or tens – to qualify for lending or credit schemes. Indubitably, it proves more profitable for lending institutions to lend money to communities of women where they can maximise their turnover irrespective of whether women are making any money from the loans: continuous recruitment and policing of group members ensure high return rates. Hence, with very little investment women become effective mediums of cash generation and multiplication.

## Women as objects or subjects of trade

In many respects, therefore, women are becoming the objects of trade. Businesses target women using both traditional and modern techniques. Economic liberalisation has seen an influx of luxury items in Tanzania, the most significant being cosmetics. Images of the modern woman championed by the media result in the dumping of cheap beauty products such as whitening creams, the health consequences of which are yet to be assessed. The promoters and chief distributors are men, while women are the willing or beleaguered consumers. Similarly, the home, the bastion of womanhood, remains the most effective sales entry point, luring women with the possibilities of stocking up on the newest and cheapest home gadgets on the market.

This is not to say that women are sitting idly by, oblivious to emerging economic opportunities under traditional and new trade regimes. Women may have been excluded from active trade but they have never shied away from trade. Indeed, in a number of African countries women are revered for their trading skills. For example, food and textile markets in West Africa are dominated by women. It is now customary, even in conservative areas, to see women traders – women running shops and bars in urban and provincial centres; women fish vendors in coastal areas, around the Great Lakes and in Zanzibar; women trading in foodstuffs and cereals in Manyara

---

*women plough back most of the earnings*
*and profits from productive activities into*
*their families instead of expanding or*
*diversifying their businesses*

---

and Mbeya; women hawking goods in Moshi and Arusha; and women transporters in Tanga and Dar es Salaam. An increasing number of women participate in national and international trade fairs, many sponsored by themselves. More and more, women are trying to build a niche for themselves in fields previously dominated by men.

Women make up a significant proportion of the 85 per cent of Tanzanians engaged in agriculture, the mainstay of the economy. They also form a sizeable percentage of the self-employed population engaged in the informal sector. Because women's economic engagement is confined to the reproductive sector – in food production or preparation, hospitality, child caring, education, beauty and hygiene, and handicrafts – areas that affirm a woman's sexual and reproductive role, they remain excluded from more lucrative productive enterprises like large-scale farming, horticulture or industry.

Even in the fastest growing sectors of the Tanzanian economy, such as mining, women are under-performing. Whereas there is an association of women miners representing the interest of a sizeable population of women in mines, few are miners or dealers in gemstones or in industries associated with mining. The bulk of the women working in mines sells food or provides sex services. Women in the tourist industry fare no better. Men dominate the most lucrative services in the sector as tour and taxi operators, travel agents, hotel owners and managers. Women assume low-ranking service jobs such as telephone operators, waitresses, chambermaids, cleaners, travel agent sales persons, and flight attendants. As is the case of women in the food industry, women in the tourist industry are pushed into prostitution to supplement meagre incomes.

# Economic success but at what price for women?

Increasing insecurity in their personal lives may make women reluctant participants in commerce. Microcredit programmes are replete with reports of husbands who appropriate loans or earnings, exacerbating women's poverty. Similarly, little attention has been paid to the great physical risk women face on account of their economic success. Economic success does not shield women from the threat of violence and a number of them experience acts of aggression on account of their business success. A case in point involves a popular female fish trader in Arusha market, Mama Terry, who was recently robbed in her home. A close male relative, jealous of her business success, paid the gangsters to 'fix her'. Thankfully, when they attacked she had a sizeable amount of cash in her possession. Distracted by the loot, the thugs left without harming her. Other women are not so lucky, falling victims to both sexual and physical violence after being gang robbed.

Clearly, women are allowed to engage in productive economic activity as long as they do not go beyond social expectations. Otherwise, relatives and society at large reserve the right to apply some form of sanction to neutralise a woman's economic mobility.

It is common for young traders, frustrated by severe economic alienation, to physically and verbally attack women they perceive as successful. They feel such women 'undermine their chances' of making it in a competitive business environment.

Sadly, models of 'women of substance' in trade and business continue to be scarce, even among female business graduates. Interestingly, women with business education end up teaching or overseeing less fortunate women in microcredit and lending programmes. Few actually venture into business. Moreover, instead of being at the forefront of an emancipatory trade and economic agenda, business professionals do very little to emancipate themselves and other women from economic bondage. Rather, they serve the dominant trade framework, becoming brokers for financial interests, urging on poor and less educated women to take on loans and subscribe to economic models that keep them on a leash of economic dependency and exploitation.

A few business-savvy women serve as self-appointed advocates for women's economic justice. They exercise vigilance over global processes that dictate the terms of trade for men and women in the global South. Nevertheless, they communicate via a language and process far removed from the realities of women they represent: Their discourse is too technical, aimed at policy makers and academics. Whereas these women could have provided the link between professionalism and creativity in local enterprise, or with local governments, their oppositional stance serves to alienate women further from entrepreneurship, seeing it as too complex and mystical a venture.

Ultimately, women continue to miss out on role models in the business world. They miss being groomed by women with a conceptual and practical understanding of the system. They remain confused and intimidated by the jargon and procedures that restrict their spontaneity to venture and risk. They remain ignorant of terms and processes they can take advantage of because there is little interest in translating these to women. As long as women's induction to trade in the region remains microscopic, microminimised and micromanaged they will remain at the margins of trading blocks, earning just enough for their survival and that of their families. How then can such a trade development formula realistically contribute to women's economic empowerment?

**Further reading**

Society for International Development (2006) 'The State of East Africa Report 2006 – Trends, Tensions and Contradictions: the Leadership Challenge'

Khadija Mohammed Hijja (2005) 'Women and tourism in Zanzibar', unpublished

# STREET VENDORS AND INFORMAL TRADING – THE STRUGGLE FOR THE RIGHT TO TRADE

## WINNIE MITULLAH

June 2006

Negotiations about international trade tend to have relevance for large firms or formal enterprises. But, asks Winnie Mitullah, what about the rights of the large number of workers in African cities involved in informal trade?

When one hears the word 'trade' what comes to mind is the large-scale formal traders, international trade organisations such as the World Trade Organisation (WTO) and regional organisations such as the Common Market for Eastern and Southern Africa (COMESA). While such traders and institutions are important, street vendors and informal trade, which provide employment and incomes to a significant percentage of people in Africa, in particular in urban areas, are hardly ever thought of.

Street and informal traders are part of the informal economy. The informal sector comprise half to three-quarters of non-agricultural employment in developing countries. These traders make up 48 per cent of non-agricultural employment in Africa, 51 per cent in Latin America, 65 per cent in Asia, and 72 per cent in sub-Saharan Africa, excluding South Africa. Employment in this sector operates without contracts, worker benefits or social protection, and most employees and individuals have no rights to organise and be represented.

The theme of the UN–HABITAT Global Campaign on good urban governance is the 'inclusive city'. The campaign advances the position that an inclusive approach must be used to balance, reconcile and trade off competing interests and priorities. In most

*The human rights organisations responsible for the clamour for rights have still to adequately specify what they mean by economic rights or adequately strategise about how to claim or enforce worker rights.*

119

cities the interests of micro and small enterprises such as street and informal traders compete with those of medium and large-scale enterprises, with the former being disadvantaged. All types of enterprises in urban areas, whether micro, small, medium or large, should have the right not only to access the central business district (CBD) but all urban goods and services. The global campaign has noted that the notion of inclusion resonates differently in each region with exclusion of specific groups being most significant in some regions and exclusion of the poor majority more important in others. The campaign urges actors to discuss the question of 'who' in a particular city is excluded from 'what' and 'how'. This article demonstrates how street and informal traders are not integrated into urban planning and development.

Concepts such as participation, empowerment and social inclusion have become buzzwords, and yet to the poor who are engaged in informal economic activities these concepts do not make much sense. When these concepts are used, emphasis is often placed on participatory development and participatory political processes, rather than

---

*The greatest challenge facing street and informal traders is their right to trading space. Most of the spaces traders occupy are considered illegal since they have not been set aside for trade.*

---

on participatory market processes. Further, the proponents of democratic practices tend to focus on political democracy to the neglect of economic democracy, while the proponents of empowerment and voice tend to focus on the individual rather than the collective. Street and informal traders have still to fully adopt joint action in dealing with urban authorities.

The human rights organisations responsible for the clamour for rights have still to adequately specify what they mean by economic rights or adequately strategise about how to claim or enforce worker rights. Even the micro-financial institutions, whose clients work mainly within the informal economy, have focused on financial services to the neglect of other business services and how the wider policy and regulatory environment affects their clients. Most vendors rely on moneylenders or informal sources of credit in order to buy their merchandise. As a result, they pay exorbitant interest rates and their businesses rarely grow beyond subsistence levels.

The Bellagio International Declaration of Street Vendors of November 1995 urged governments to develop national policies for hawkers and vendors which would improve their standards of living. This could be done by giving street traders legal status, issuing them with licences and providing appropriate hawking zones in urban areas. The declaration further called on governments to integrate vendors into urban development plans. Since then, a number of global, regional and local associations have been established to protect the rights of street and informal traders. The global networks include Women in Informal Employment Globalising and Organising (WIEGO), with a secretariat at Harvard University in the USA, and StreetNet International, with headquarters in Durban, South Africa. StreetNet has regional and local networks which have begun engaging urban authorities in policy dialogues on issues such as the right to trade in urban space.

Street vending and informal trade is spreading rapidly in the cities of most developing countries and is a source of employment and income to a large percentage of urban households. The trade takes place at strategic points where there is heavy human traffic – along main roads, in parks, on pavements, within shopping centres and at street and road junctions where traders are visible to pedestrians and motorists. The traders use different means to display their goods, including mats, gunny bags, tables, racks, wheelbarrows, handcarts and bicycle seats. Some traders simply carry their commodities on their hands, heads and shoulders, while others hang their goods on walls, trees and fences. An advanced but numerically insignificant group of traders construct temporary shades with stands for displaying their goods.

## Challenges of trade

The greatest challenge facing street and informal traders is their right to trading space. Most of the spaces traders occupy are considered illegal since they have not been set aside for trade. Where they are allowed to operate, the spaces are considered to be temporary and eviction occurs at the will of urban authorities. Major conflict often arises when the vendors are required to move in order to give way for planned development. This brings them into direct confrontation with urban authorities and land developers. Most of the spaces the traders occupy have no tenure and are not allocated and sanctioned by urban authorities. At the same time, the traders are also in conflict with formal shop owners and landlords, who contend that the traders infringe on their businesses and/or premises.

The spaces occupied by traders are in the open and leave them vulnerable to the weather. Most of the commodities they trade in such as fruit, vegetables and clothes are damaged by the harsh environmental conditions, which means a loss of earnings for the traders. Overall, it has been noted that street vendors and informal traders are perhaps the most regulated and least protected. They trade illegally because they are not recognised and have no licences. The traders are known to identify trading sites on their own, leaving the urban authorities with few options other than to evict them, tolerate them or charge them a daily fee without providing any legal protection.

When they are evicted, the traders are often given the option of a site outside the central business district where there are hardly any customers. This option is based on an exclusion framework that reserves the central business district for large-scale traders and businesses, which urban authorities argue pay taxes unlike the street vendors and informal traders. This argument is false: research has shown that when both daily fees and bribes to urban authorities are taken into consideration, the urban authori-

---

*The poor, in particular street and informal traders, are disadvantaged in trade at global, regional and local levels. Under pressure from rich countries, the barriers to international trade in goods and financial services and investment flows have been lowered to the advantage of capital over labour and of large firms over small and micro firms.*

---

ties collect more from traders than they need. Research has further shown that daily fee charges are more expensive than a lump sum payment for a licence. However, the street and informal traders make minimal profit and are not able to make lump sum payments.

The lack of a street trading licence exposes traders to harassment and punitive measures, including confiscation of goods. After losing the goods in which their capital is tied, some traders have to close their businesses. Research in a number of African cities reveals that having a licence does not guarantee safety and recognition by the urban authorities. In most cases, vendors are not issued with any identification that shows they have a legitimate right to sell their goods in urban streets. This exposes them to harassment, including confiscation of goods, assault and demands for bribes.

Until the dawn of governance reform programmes in Africa, licences were largely commodities of trade, peddled by either urban authority officials or those who had access to the urban authorities. This was an outcome of the planning laws, which do not take into account the existence of street vendors and informal traders. Most urban plans locate the traders, without any consultation, in the peripheral areas of the city where there is no business. Experience across Africa shows that traders never stick to such areas. They drift back to the centre, resulting in punitive measures from the city authorities. Most of the policies and regulations being enforced on street and market traders owe their origin to colonial policies, which did not favour small-scale local enterprises. Street and informal traders require laws that recognise their economic activities as an important component of the urban economy, and ensure their right to trading space.

## An insecure environment

Apart from the right to trading space, street and informal traders are also disadvantaged in the area of security, transport and municipal services. A secure working environment is a prerequisite for any type of business and a major concern for many people engaged in economic activities on the streets. Municipal authorities have been the major source of insecurity for these traders. The authorities harass and beat street vendors and confiscate their goods without any warning. This threatens not only vendors but also their customers. A study of cities in South Africa has noted that an insecure environment results in loss of customers, frightens tourists, cripples business, reduces incomes and generally interferes with trading.

The insecurity in the streets is sometimes used as an excuse for evicting street traders. In many cities in Africa, street trading sites are viewed by urban authorities as dens for thugs and robbers. In 2001 the Kampala city authority used an increase in city theft and insecurity as grounds for evicting vendors from the streets. While it may be true that criminals mingle with traders, an assumption that the informal traders are criminals is part of a scheme by urban elites to exclude them from the benefits of operating in the developed areas of cities. A rights perspective requires urban authorities to identify and deal with culprits as opposed to condemning a whole sector of an urban economy.

Most vendors find it difficult to transport their goods from their homes and markets to their trading sites. This is because most transport systems do not service the areas where vendors live. Where they do, the vendors can barely afford the service. In some cases, there are restrictions on what an individual can take on the bus, mini-bus or train. This forces vendors to carry their goods on their backs or to hire handcarts or human carriers to transport their goods. This is complicated further by lack of storage facilities, which means the traders have to carry the unsold goods back to their homes.

Other basic services are also not available to vendors and consumers. Apart from a few cities in South Africa, street and informal traders operate without access to water and sanitation. A few of them use services from neighbouring formal markets, hotels and bars while the majority rely on unsafe water sources, unsanitary methods of refuse disposal and the use of open spaces for sanitary facilities. Others obtain services from their homes or nearby residential areas. Municipal cleansing services are inadequate and do not cover informal trading areas, nor do the urban authorities facilitate the provision of services by traders and other stakeholders. In cases where traders are organised, they clean their sites of operation or hire people to collect and dispose garbage.

The poor, in particular street and informal traders, are disadvantaged in trade at global, regional and local levels. Under pressure from rich countries, the barriers to international trade in goods and financial services and investment flows have been lowered to the advantage of capital over labour and of large firms over small and micro firms. The negative trade and policy processes largely disadvantage the wage-workers and own account producers in the informal economy, and yet they are the majority poor who are the focus of current policies and development processes. The neglect of micro and small traders has to be reversed if African countries are to change existing poverty trends.

# FRIEND OR FOE – THE EPAS UNMASKED

**LIEPOLLO LEBOHANG PHEKO**

January 2007

Liepollo Lebohang Pheko discusses the real impact of the economic partnership agreements (EPAs) on women and the failures of liberalisation policies to examine and address the specific needs of women.

Trade liberalisation produces different results for men and women. The differential outcomes are associated with the most essential aspects of livelihoods and well-being, including food security, employment, income and access to affordable health services. Different outcomes across countries and regions depend on the economic area and specific sector, the measures introduced, and the timing and sequencing of trade policies. The effects of trade liberalisation are felt across areas as diverse as agriculture, services, clothing and textiles, and intellectual property.

Policy makers and any groups concerned with gender equality, poverty eradication and development-orientated economic growth must be aware of the massive constraints and challenges presented by the liberalisation of these sectors. In short any cultural, policy and structural constructs that ignore or exacerbate the oppression of women must be redrafted or replaced.

The EPAs have not examined the cost of liberalisation for women in terms of physical resources, human resources, the social capital needed to transfer resources, and the skills to effectively manage liberalisation. The liberalisation programme of EPAs need to be examined in a broader, gendered context that is mindful of the non-neutrality of the market economy.

## The geopolitics of EPAs

It is crucial to be mindful of the geopolitical agenda which propels the EPAs. These agreements are being punted at a time when European markets are shrinking, production costs are making it difficult for companies to make a significant profit from Northern consumers and three successive World Trade Organisation (WTO) ministerial meetings have gone badly for corporate interests.

The African, Caribbean and the Pacific (ACP) countries offer the opportunity for the European Union (EU) to find an unfettered market. Many observers thus argue that the EU's intentions are related more to pro-North market driven interests than pro-South development ones.

*The need for flexible workers to respond to market fluctuations has led to a rise in the numbers of informal sector workers, of which a high percentage are women.*

This assertion is evidenced by the intensity of protectionism the EU is permitted while habitually dumping surplus produce on overseas markets. Though 90 per cent of ACP countries' tariffs must be removed to access EU markets, there is no mention of dismantling the Common Agricultural Policy or of stemming the anti-competitive practices that arise from dumping. The consensus among many progressives, NGOs and policy analysts in both the South and North is that there is great cause for concern.

## EPAs and women

In all this, women emerge as the double losers. THE EPAs focus on primary production and force countries to de-industrialise. As such:

- Women are locked into the lowest paid work with the least statutory protection and benefits. Even though employment may increase, the quality of that employment is poor.
- Labour rights are thus violated while factories are given tax holidays at the expense of providing real livelihoods and permanent employment to women workers.
- Women are forced to compete with poorly paid contract workers abroad as the move to 'outsourcing' continues, as seen in the notorious export processing zones (EPZs) operating in the South.
- The ability to organise and gather as unions or worker groups is minimised through threats, bullying and, in extreme cases, the murder of vocal workers.
- Women's reproductive rights are violated whether through forced abortions, dismissal when pregnancy is disclosed, or miscarriages through strenuous work and exposure to toxic chemicals
- Earning an income outside the home can lead to greater empowerment for women, both in the household and in the wider community. However, trade liberalisation can also lead to unemployment and the restructuring of labour markets – a situation that tends to affect poor and marginalised groups of women

more than men. In fact, occupational and wage segregation is widening and bad working conditions are rife in many export industries. The need for flexible workers to respond to market fluctuations has led to a rise in the numbers of informal sector workers, of which a high percentage are women.

- Access to education, healthcare and other basic services is often truncated through trade liberalisation. There is often less to spend at household level so the role of social reproduction in terms of providing care, gathering fuel and food, etc, falls upon the women and girls. Where choices are made about whether to send the boy or girl child to school, most communities and families favour the boy. The 'care economy' meanwhile remains unregulated and unsupported;
- The displacement of indigenous women farmers and artisans in favour of facilities for European tourism is transforming the South into a huge exotic safari park, often linked with an increasing sex trade.
- The diminishing of women's role as custodians of traditional knowledge and biodiversity has been well documented and bears restating in the wake of the GM assault and the threat to food sovereignty.
- Cheaper goods enter national markets from overseas, affecting existing indigenous producers but also providing cheaper options for consumers, many of whom are women who manage diminishing household budgets.

## Value added tax and women

Value added tax (VAT) can be extremely unfavourable for women, not only as consumers but also in relation to their reproductive role, since it is normally levied on household goods and labour-saving devices such as domestic appliances. This is in addition to the taxes paid on food at the point of purchase.

The theory of fiscal austerity has fundamental repercussions for expenditure on services such as health and education, which are critical particularly for women in their socially assigned task as 'carers'. Fiscal austerity may also constrict governments' capacity to establish social protection measures and safety nets to counteract the harmful consequences of liberalisation.

## Production structures and employment

In real terms, the effects and shocks of trade are experienced by individual women, by individual men, by households, by families and by communities whenever fluctuations in price (related to availability of goods) and changes in output (the goods and services people work to produce, how they produce them and under what conditions) occur. A typical claim made by advocates of EPA policies, including some gender advocates, is that increased trade and investment liberalisation can improve economic growth, which in turn can increase women's participation in the labour market. However, we need to examine the nature and terms of this participation.

The rapid liberalisation of tariffs in the South African footwear and leather industry (from 41.2 per cent in 1995 to 28.9 per cent in 1999) has resulted in the loss of jobs and

---

*The displacement of indigenous women farmers and artisans in favour of facilities for European tourism is transforming the South into a huge exotic safari park, often linked with an increasing sex trade.*

---

drastic changes in production processes in local factories.

Additionally, there is a correlation between company restructuring in the footwear industry and the expansion of the informal sector. Not only is this the only apparent option for the increasing number of unemployed workers, but also for factories, which subcontract to the informal sector in order to cut labour costs. South Africa's informal sector has increased from 1,136,000 workers in 1997 to 1,907,000 in 1999. There are approximately 193,000 African women compared to 28,000 white women working in the informal sector. What this illustrates is that it is the social groups with the least power and resources who are over represented in the 'informal' sector.

## Investment measures

There are typically four ways in which a government can protect the environment of national investment measures:

- By prescribing and enforcing minimum local content requirements (in terms of value, volume or proportion)
- By setting trade balancing requirements (limits on purchase or use of an imported product up to the maximum value or volume related to local production)
- By placing restrictions on repatriation of dividends
- By placing ceilings on the equity holding of foreign investors.

Several African, Caribbean, South American and Asian countries have adjusted their mercantile and investment laws to comply with bilateral investment agreements aimed at encouraging foreign direct investment (FDI). Usually the result has been to remove regulations which govern minimum local content, trade balancing, access to foreign exchange and repatriation of dividends.

Several South American and Asian countries implemented import substitution policies in the 1960s and 1970s to encourage local production of consumer goods and to maintain a balance of payments through barriers on certain imports. Under WTO agreements these would now be illegal. The gender dimensions of this are that women tend to work more in industries in which capital flight is common and that are more susceptible to foreign competition. These industries are profoundly distressed by economic downturns, which have repercussions on the job protection of the largely female workforce.

Some years ago, the Senegalese government reduced tariffs on food imports to

---

*Women tend to work more in industries in which capital flight is common and that are more susceptible to foreign competition. These industries are profoundly distressed by economic downturns, which have repercussions on the job protection of the largely female workforce.*

---

comply with a trade liberalisation package. This coincided with the launch of a tomato paste business by a group of Senegalese women. They had taken out microcredit loans. Once they had shifted from producing subsistence crops to solely growing tomatoes, the tariffs dropped and cheap foreign tomatoes flooded the Senegalese market. In what seems the typical story of the South when confronted with Northern imports, cooperatives were unable to compete. The result was that they could not honour the payment of microcredit loans. This illustrates the hostility of the market towards women and less resourced business people. It also shows the importance of Southern government regulation and protectionism of women and their families. It is critical to prevent families from entering economic situations that are more invidious than before as a result of placing them in competitive environments without adequate support.

## Women entrepreneurs

Enterprise development and market access are commonly promoted as policies that enable developing countries to engage in international trade. Overall, liberalisation under the WTO rules has not significantly increased women's access to credit, nor has it enhanced opportunities to generate domestic savings for entrepreneurial activities. Structural gender inequalities linked to property rights and ownership mean that women have fewer assets that can serve as collateral.

Instead of introducing a framework to enable women's access to credit and venture capital, profit-motivated liberalisation policies have propagated the discrimination against marginalised and dispossessed women by mainstream financial markets by aiming at urban areas and more lucrative economic sectors. This excludes poor women, who are concentrated in the informal sector and operate mostly in small and medium enterprises. The most favoured nation principle merely enforces this.

Women largely go to unregulated sources of venture capital, such as specialised moneylenders, pawnbrokers, savings and credit associations. These are characterised by their lack of regulation and high interest rates.

## Currency devaluation

Currency devaluations have particularly insidious effects on people living on the economic margins, especially women. Typically, women and girls absorb the direct consequence of price increases because of the classic expectations that women are the custodians of domestic well-being. This means they take on extra paid and unpaid workloads to outpace appreciating prices; adopt survival mechanisms to source affordable alternatives (such as replacing home produced food for shop bought); and they transfer limited food rations to family members who earn the most.

The African Women Leaders in Agriculture and Environment (AWLAE) have published a case study of the devaluation of the CFA franc in Mali. The findings assert that since the devaluation, 'women are participating in greater numbers in agricultural production as the number of households threatened by food insecurity increases'. Women invested more labour in cultivating crops to generate more income. This meant they had less time for childcare at home. In addition AWLAE's research also exposed the irony that women's status improved as a result of their 'indispensable' financial contributions to the household. With an inverse coping strategy, the men tended to abandon their social, community and household responsibilities as financial pressures mounted.

## Capital controls on direct investment

Capital controls (owning physical property) or portfolio investment (investing in the stock and bond market) are pivotal in preventing speculative investment and encourage enhanced financial stability. Speculative investment often results in major economic disturbance, and swift, substantial changes in money moving into or out of a country for rapid profit. Investment controls restrict external money flows, enabling countries to pursue social investment priorities such as employment creation and technology transfer. Free market proponents argue that liberal capital movement is more efficient while restrictions discourage investment. The primary concern of the free market investment environment is that investors may opt to go to countries with fewer controls.

A good case study is provided by the Asian financial crisis, a major catalyst of which was the swift flight of capital from Thailand, Indonesia, and Korea, following a dras-

## Facts and figures: women's rights and trade

'A 2002 REPORT by the International Labor Rights Fund (ILRF) documents violence against women in agricultural industries in Kenya. Many women harvesting coffee and tea for export have kept silent about extreme sexual harassment—even rape—by their supervisors in order to keep their jobs.'
*http://www.laborrights.org/publications/ tradewomen1202.pdf#search=%22statistics%20on%20 trade%20and%20women's%20rights%22*

* * * * * * * * * * * * * * * * * * * * * * * *

'98 PER CENT OF WEALTH on earth is in the hands of men, and only 2 per cent belongs to women.'
*http://www.whrnet.org/docs/issue- globalisation.html#Facts*

* * * * * * * * * * * * * * * * * * * * * * * *

'SOME 70–90 PER CENT of the workers employed in export processing zones (EPZs) are women. Women also produce more than half of the world's household goods and their share of informal employment generally matches or exceeds men's.'
*http://www.wto.org/English/tratop_e/dda_e/ symp03_gwit_e.doc*

* * * * * * * * * * * * * * * * * * * * * * * *

'THE 225 RICHEST "persons" in the world, who are men, own the same capital as the 2,500 million poorest people. Of these 2,500 million poorest people, 80 per cent are women.'
*http://www.whrnet.org/docs/issue-globalisation. html#Facts*

* * * * * * * * * * * * * * * * * * * * * * * *

'IN SENEGAL, TOMATO PRODUCTION used to provide rural households with a good living. But after liberalisation, the prices farmers received for their tomatoes halved, and tomato production fell from 73,000 tonnes in 1990 to just 20,000 tonnes in 1997.'
*http://www.awid.org/go.php?list=analysis&prefix=ana lysis&item=00264*

'THIRTEEN COUNTRIES – of which Burundi, Liberia, Nigeria, Somalia and Tanzania are a few – are in the same shape or worse off today than they were in 1990. For almost 40 countries the data is insufficient to say anything, which probably reflects an even worse situation for women.'
*Social Watch, an NGO watchdog system http://www. twnside.org.sg/title/height.htm*

* * * * * * * * * * * * * * * * * * * * * * * *

'WOMEN ARE INCREASINGLY AT RISK of working in highly exploitative and dangerous conditions because trade liberalisation tends to increase their employment in the industrial sector, in commercial agriculture and in export processing zones, which are characterised by low rates of pay and sub-standard conditions.'
*http://www.awid.org/publications/primers/ factsissues4.pdf*

* * * * * * * * * * * * * * * * * * * * * * * *

'ONE OF THE BIGGEST PROBLEMS with many economic policies is their failure to account for women's unpaid work. For many women, unpaid work, (including attending to children, cooking and small-scale farming) accounts for a large portion of their contribution to the economy.'
*http://www.awid.org/publications/primers/ factsissues6.pdf*

* * * * * * * * * * * * * * * * * * * * * * * *

'[T]HERE IS GROWING EVIDENCE that trade liberalisation tends to disadvantage women, who constitute the majority of small-scale farmers in rural areas. According to the FAO, women make up about 44 per cent of the formally documented agricultural work force in developing countries'
*http://www.cid.harvard.edu/cidtrade/Papers/gibb. pdf#search=%22statistics%20on%20trade%20and%20 women's%20rights%22*

September 2006

tic increase in speculation. (Foreign direct investment had doubled in South Korea, Indonesia, Malaysia, Thailand and the Philippines between 1994 and1996.) Most of these countries had inadequate (if any) capital controls having liberalised financial markets without sufficient regulations. This inadequately protected environment enabled investors and well-off individuals to effortlessly remove money from banks, the stock market and certain businesses to more lucrative off-shore markets. Inexorably, financial volatility resulting from capital flight led to plummeting foreign exchange rates, triggered scores of bankruptcies and momentarily shattered Asian economies.

This period was characterised by escalating joblessness and rising prices for essential commodities. The numbers of people in extreme poverty soared in tandem with the increasingly desperate economic conditions. For example from 1997 to 1998, unemployment in Indonesia tripled, according to the International Labour Organisation. One immediate coping mechanism was to despatch women and girls to augment household incomes. Indonesian government figures state that there was an increase of 2.4 million self-employed people and 1.3 million in unpaid workers (including in family businesses such as farms). It is not clear how many of new workers were female. What is well documented is that females are disproportionately over-represented in the informal sector and among unpaid family workers. Statistical data is not yet able to quantify the spectacular rise in migrant labour and prostitution among Indonesian women.

## Conclusion

The EPAs will undeniably affect individuals, families and communities through their impact on prices, employment, capital flows, investment conditions and production structures. Most critics of the EPAs agree that these structural changes will have differentiated consequences on women and men, the wealthiest and the least wealthy due to their different positions in the economic system. These diverse positions arise partly from various national contexts and are strengthened by nuanced social and cultural factors such as gender, ethnicity, class or race. Furthermore, the 'new issues' put forward by the WTO, which have so far been resisted, could make a pernicious comeback through the EPAs.

In all this the power and social relations between the South and the North, between women and men, between girls and boys, between differently abled citizens, between the economically dispossessed and the wealthy, between people with different educational attainments, and a plethora of other societal textures will be exacerbated. The experiences of economic structural adjustment programmes and the current struggles against the WTO provide ample evidence of this.

The EPAs have implications for job security, livelihoods, well-being and human rights. The dangers of liberalisation for women are crystallised by the construct of social inclusion. This inherently respects and acknowledges a sense of human community in which all community interests must be considered in order for the whole to progress.

These bring human rights to life and remind us that any policy, practice or law that further removes the displaced, further excludes the marginalised and further impoverishes the most vulnerable – most of whom are women – must be redrafted, rethought and realigned to promote gender equity and authentic social transformation.

This paper was presented at the European Commission, Brussels, and is republished here with the kind permission of the author.

Trade, environment and agriculture

# TRADE AND HUMAN RIGHTS IN THE NIGER DELTA
## NNIMMO BASSEY
June 2006

The Niger Delta has been described as 'exploited, misused, abused, polluted, underdeveloped, and almost completely dead; like a cherry fruit sucked and discarded'.[1] Nnimmo Bassey looks at the crude oil trade in the Niger Delta and finds it is anything but sweet for local communities.

The Niger Delta of Nigeria has been in the news so repeatedly that the issues merit little introduction. In one sense the issues are a mesh of politics, trade and resource exploitation. All these work to gravely undermine the rights of people to protection against the exploitation of their natural environment.

The Niger Delta is the treasure base of Nigeria, since successive governments have decided to ignore the other sustainable income sources that supported the nation before the discovery of oil in commercial quantities. Today, according to official counts, oil contributes about 95 per cent of the country's foreign exchange earnings from the production of 2.2 million barrels of crude per day. An additional chunk is extracted illegally into private and corporate pockets through crude oil bunkering. These all lead to the milking of the Niger Delta to the point of near death. The area suffers from a dearth of social amenities, high unemployment, environmental degradation and social malaise.

Oil corporations such as Shell and Chevron, who are major players in the Niger Delta, have admitted to contributing to corruption, violence and civil unrest in the Niger Delta. In Shell's 'Peace and security' report (published in 2003) as well as Chevron's double page ads in Nigerian newspapers in May 2005, the corporations admit that by their actions they have contributed to the state of conflict, corruption and distortion in both the Niger Delta environment and by extension the Nigerian state.

According to the Shell report:

Annual casualties from fighting already place the Niger Delta in the 'high intensity conflict' category (over 1,000 fatalities a year), alongside better known cases such as Chechnya and Colombia. The criminalisation and political economy of conflicts in the region mean that the basis for escalated, protracted and entrenched violence is rapidly being established. This not only threatens SCIN's (Shell Companies in Nigeria) future ability to operate, but also Nigerian national security.[2]

Trade has remained the major precursor of destruction in the Niger Delta. We can go right back to trade practices where highly valuable goods were exchanged for bottles of whisky, beads and mirrors, or to the days during which the Niger Delta lost human resources through the slave trade. Before the advent of the crude oil trade in the Niger Delta, we have it on record that on 22 February 1895 the trading city, Brass, located here, was attacked and levelled by British naval forces at the behest of the Royal Niger

---

*Trade has remained the major precursor of destruction in the Niger Delta. We can go right back to trade practices where highly valuable goods were exchanged for bottles of whisky, beads and mirrors, or to the days during which the Niger Delta lost human resources through the slave trade.*

---

Company to ensure that the company had a monopoly over the palm oil trade for which the town was famous. Over 2,000 persons, mostly women and children, lost their lives in that attack.

In modern times, it has been said that since Shell arrived in the Niger Delta the tale has been one of desolation. Much of the activity in the Niger Delta surrounding crude oil and its exploitation involves rights abuses – as the world learnt from the struggles of Ken Saro-Wiwa and the Ogoni people and the subsequent hanging of Saro-Wiwa.

## Unending horrors

There is an unending story of horrors coming out of the Niger Delta. Oil spills and pipeline fires are regular features; according to official estimates there are at least 300 incidents each year. Clean-up exercises are spade and shovel jobs. Capping off of the leaks often sets the remaining crude oil on fire. In this way forests and even rivers have been set ablaze. These crude oil spills poison the land, pollute water bodies and expose the people to untold hardship. Consider also the response to communities attempting to protect their rights:

- In 1990, the Umuechem community was visited by contingents of the Nigerian police. Eighty community members were murdered in the unprovoked attack.

Houses were burnt down or looted. The people of Umuechem had been engaged in peaceful protests at the gates of the Shell flow station in their community.[3]

- On 10 November 1995, the Nigerian military regime of General Sani Abacha murdered Ken Saro-Wiwa and eight other leaders of the Ogoni people in the Niger Delta after a kangaroo tribunal set up by the regime convicted them on trumped up charges of murder. The world responded with outrage. The Ogoni had started peaceful protests in 1993 against the destruction of their natural environment and livelihoods.

- For the people of Ilaje community, in Nigeria's Ondo state, 28 May 1998 is a day they will not forget. Ilaje youths had occupied Chevron's oil platform in an attempt to persuade Chevron to talk with them. The Nigerian military and police swooped down on the young protestors in helicopters. Reports have it that the attackers were shooting as they landed, Rambo style, killing two youths on the spot.[4] A lawsuit about this is currently being heard in San Francisco, USA.

- On 20 November 1999, barely six months into his first term as civilian president of Nigeria, President Obasanjo ordered soldiers into Odi, a town in the Niger Delta. By the time they left, the destruction of the town was complete and 2,483 people had been slain. The dead included women, children and the elderly and infirm.[5]

- About 50 members of the Odioma community in Bayelsa state were reported massacred on Saturday 19 February 2005 during a military raid by a joint task force of the Nigerian army and navy.[6] The soldiers also destroyed the whole community, with houses bombed and burnt in a manner reminiscent of the Odi massacre of 1999. Again, those killed were mostly women, children and the elderly. Odioma community, located in Brass local government area of Bayelsa state, is one of the many communities in the Niger Delta with oil in their land They had been in conflict with the neighbouring Bassambri community over the ownership of a fishing settlement where Shell has some oil wells. Shell planned to build an oil flow station at Obioku and had actually mobilised its contractors to start work on the site from 20 January 2005. Work on the project was stopped by protesting youths from the Odioma community because of the lack of an enviromental impact assessment.

## Gas flaring

In addition to the vigorous protests by communities, the struggle for human rights was given a boost on 14 November 2005 when a high court sitting in Benin City ruled that the practice of flaring gas, associated with crude oil extraction, was an infringement of the fundamental human rights of the people living in the communities where the flaring is carried out. The judge subsequently ordered that the top guns of Shell and the Nigeria National Petroleum Corporation (NNPC) should appear before him to show a clear step by step plan for stopping gas flaring a year from that date. This and other gas flare cases have been filed by communities with the collaboration of

Environmental Rights Action (ERA) (Friends of the Earth Nigeria) as well as the Climate Justice Programme.

Gas flaring has been going on in the Niger Delta for close to 50 years and has been estimated to constitute a waste of $2.5 billion annually. Besides being an economic waste, the flares release a cocktail of toxic and greenhouse gases into the atmosphere and greatly endanger the lives of people. Health problems associated with gas flares

---

*As long as the trade booms, respect for rights will remain elusive. It is this realisation which appears to form the bedrock of the local people's insistence that there should be community control over community resources.*

---

include respiratory diseases, cancer, acute nonlymphocytic leukemia and a variety of other blood-related disorders. The environmental problems, including acid rain and damage to water bodies and farms, are no less horrendous.

The government and Chevron, who are the project executors of the West African Gas Pipeline project (WAGP), plan to harvest and pipe liquefied natural gas from new gas fields in Escravos in the Niger Delta to industrial complexes in Benin, Togo and Ghana. They have been presenting it as an answer to the gas flaring problem. They also present the WAGP as a clean development mechanism project in order to claim carbon credits.

The truth, however, is that the project has nothing to do with ending or reducing gas flaring in the Niger Delta because a huge proportion of the gas it would convey would only be harvested from gas fields as opposed to being associated gas. Communities affected by this project have sent a petition to the inspection panel of the World Bank, claiming that many rules of the bank have been flouted in the project and that their rights are not respected. Indeed, the local communities in the firing lines of this project have rejected the scheme and insist that decisions have been made without first conducting the necessary environmental, social and other impact assessments. The WAGP is emblematic of the rape of the Niger Delta by transnational corporations and collaborating governments. Projects and trade decisions are made without regard to the rights of the people.

But as the oil wells begin to run dry, the competition is getting more acute. The Chinese are making bold grabs for the oil fields of the Niger Delta. The USA sees the region as being of critical strategic interest. TheWorld Bank and the Paris Club eye the petrodollars coming into the region as theirs for the taking. All these combine to make the future of the region more precarious. With growing resistance in the region it is anyone's guess how things will play out.

*Gas flaring has been going on in the Niger Delta for close to 50 years and has been estimated to constitute a waste of $2.5 billion annually. Besides being an economic waste, the flares release a cocktail of toxic and greenhouse gases into the atmosphere and greatly endanger the lives of people.*

As long as the trade booms, respect for rights will remain elusive. It is this realisation which appears to form the bedrock of the local people's insistence that there should be community control over community resources. They reckon that this would enable them to decide whether they wanted any mineral in their environment to be exploited. And when they did, they would b able to ensure that their rights were respected and that benefits from exploitation wuld accrue to them.

It is conceivable that the refusal of the state to accept this proposition is the trigger to the present conflagration in the Niger Delta. Another growing demand among environmentalists such as those in the Oilwatch International network is that there should be a moratorium on new oil explorations for, say, ten years. The intervening time would be used to make an audit of the pollution and abuses that have accumulated over the years, commence clean-up and remediation actions and decide how the vulnerable communities would fare in a post-petroleum economy when they would be left with nothing but a polluted environment.

**Notes**

1 Quoted in Terisa E. Turner and Leigh S. Brownhill (2003) '"Why women are at war with Chevron" Nigerian subsistence struggles against the international oil industry'. New York: International Oil Working Group <http://www.uoguelph.ca/~terisat/un.htm>.

2 Shell Petroleum Development Company of Nigeria (SPDC) (2003) 'Peace and security in the Niger Delta: Conflict Expert Group baseline report', SPD.

3 Environmental Rights Action (ERA) (2005) *The Shell Report*. Benin City, Nigeria: ERA <http://www.eraction.org/modules/Publications/docs/shellreport.pdf>.

# COMMUNITY RIGHTS AND FOREIGN DIRECT INVESTMENT IN KENYA'S YALA SWAMP

## PATRICK OCHIENG

June 2006

An environmentally sensitive wetland, a multinational company and a local community that feels sidelined. Sound familiar? Patrick Ochieng introduces the Yala Swamp region in Kenya and asks if foreign direct investment is really the answer to Africa's development problems.

The Yala Swamp is a wetland in western Kenya bounded to the north by the Nzoia river and to the south by the Yala river. The swampland covers an area of about 17,500 hectares (ha) in Siaya, Bondo and Busia districts that is home to nearly 1.2 million people. This is Kenya's largest wetland, a very delicate ecosystem, and the habitat of some rare flora and fauna, including endangered fish species. The swamp serves the adjacent communities as a source of fish, water, agricultural land, pastures, wild animals, plants for constructing houses, source of wood fuel and medicinal plants.

Dominion Farms Ltd, an affiliate of the USA-based Dominion Group, based in Oklahoma, USA moved into the swamp through an arrangement with the Lake Basin Development Authority (LBDA). Dominion Group controls investments across the globe. The company has businesses spanning several countries including operating luxury corporate hotels, constructing houses and offices to be leased by the US government, sportswear manufacturing and running correctional services.

The initial proposal was that Dominion would engage in rice production in part of the swamp covering about 2,300 ha. This land had been reclaimed before 1970, and had previously been farmed by LBDA. Dominion embarked on large-scale agricultural activity in the swamp following the signing of a memorandum of understanding with Siaya and Bondo councils in May 2003.

Although the rice for which the lease was executed has not been planted, the firm has engaged in activities beyond agriculture, including constructing irrigation dykes and weirs, an airstrip and a road and drilling for water. Dominion has further proposed a multi-faceted new development project within the Yala Swamp. For this purpose it is proposing that part of 9,200 ha will be reclaimed from the swamp area to meet the needs of new projects. This would leave only 6,000 ha (35 per cent) of the current wetland to act as a buffer zone.

The proposed project is extensive and specifically seeks to: implement a highly mechanised irrigation and dry farming project; construct fishponds for aquaculture; construct a fish-processing plant to process about 20 tons of fish per day, mainly for

---

*But the environmental impact assessment did not deal with the impact of the project on the soils, water quality, vegetation and wildlife. It did not deal conclusively with environmental, ecological, socio-economic and management issues related to the swamp.*

---

export; and construct a rice mill, feed mill, ginnery, fuel storage, dispensing station, turbine for electricity production, barrier dyke, weir and reservoir.

Under Kenyan law, the proposed project requires an environmental impact assessment (EIA). The EIA report submitted by Dominion consultants has concluded that:

- The project will bring into productive use a high potential resource that has been underutilised and which has cost the government and the people of Kenya huge amounts of money with few appreciable returns
- The proposed project will create employment both directly and indirectly for thousands of people through primary and secondary activities
- The project will make a positive impact on increasing incomes and meeting basic needs
- The project will act as a growth pole around which other commercial activities will gravitate
- The local communities support the proposed project, which they see as a boost to the development of the region
- The local communities are enthusiastic about the project.

But the EIA did not deal with the impact of the project on the soils, water quality, vegetation and wildlife. It did not deal conclusively with environmental, ecological, socio-economic and management issues related to the swamp. The impact of the project on water, vegetation, habitat and human activity was also not addressed. The community feels that they have not been properly consulted, and while communities were asked to form groups so that individuals did not dominate the process, this has not happened.

The consultants who carried out the EIA were employees of LBDA and thus were compromised by a conflict of interest. The sticky issue of compensation for families displaced by the project has refused to go away. Existing fish processing plants and a fishmeal plant in the area are operating below their capacity, raising the question of why it is necessary to build further plants.

## Negative impacts

The EIA report has aimed to justify the project on the basis of its economic importance, components, design, choice of location and implementation strategy and the mitigation measures put in place. The report has, however, recognised that the proposed projects will have a number of negative impacts at various stages of implementation. This list is long and some of the items will have very serious consequences. They include: flooding and altered water flow patterns; contamination of soil and water by oil leakages and spillage; pollution of the Yala river by solid and liquid waste from project activities; the possibility of respiratory ailments from inhaling dust and fumes from construction equipment; loss of grazing land for the local community; water-

---

*These export-led growth strategies subordinate human needs and human rights to corporate greed and corporate profit. Big business can never be part of a progressive and sustainable earth. Despotism and corruption have been at the core of Kenya's engagement with foreign investors.*

---

borne and vector-borne diseases; the displacement of local communities; the displacement of fauna and the loss of flora; reduced production of subsistence crops leading to food deficits in the region; and the introduction of foreign crops and genetically modified crops that may introduce new pests into the area.

At a meeting convened on 8 November 2005, we asked members of the affected communities to identify the problems the project posed for them. These included denial of access to water and land; denial of fishing rights; blocking of direct routes between communities used for trading; wage reductions; and threats of flooding as a result of dyke construction.

The community members felt that the project should be halted so that proper consultation could take place to iron out issues that had not been attended to. These include the issuing of title deeds to people whose land had been surveyed, construction only on the land that was earmarked and open discussions between the local administration, the firm, the LBDA and the community. Despite these concerns the members of parliament from the region have turned a deaf ear to the people's pleas.

There is therefore urgent need to examine, from the accounts, opinions and experiences of the different stakeholders, the socio-economic dimensions of the proposed activities. Such an independent study would inform the advocacy processes being carried out by the Friends of Yala Swamp, a loose coalition of social justice institutions, advocates and members of the affected communities who have come together to oppose the Dominion project. It would provide factual data that could help raise the stakes in negotiations with the company. It would also sharpen awareness and inform Kenya's future engagements with foreign direct investments. The study would contribute to research that will facilitate a planned court injunction to stop Dominion activities until the issues raised are addressed.

## Concerns about policy

The Yala Swamp issue raises broader concerns over government economic policy. Successive governments in Kenya have expressed a commitment to eradicate poverty in all its forms. The latest anti-poverty rhetoric is the NARC government's framework 'economic recovery for wealth creation and employment', whose central feature is anchored in the belief that foreign exchange and foreign direct investment are the solutions to Kenya's development woes. Therefore, as a country we have set out to woo foreign investors. This is despite the fact that private operators and mega projects are not accountable to the public and principally concern themselves with cost recovery and profit before anything else.

These export-led growth strategies subordinate human needs and human rights to corporate greed and corporate profit. Big business can never be part of a progressive and sustainable earth. Despotism and corruption have been at the core of Kenya's engagement with foreign investors. Compromised political elites, who are often tempted to act as stewards of imperialist interests, have continued to give away the rights to mineral exploration, fisheries, forests and forest products, biological resources and coastal biodiversity to multinationals. The Dominion Group ventures fall into this category and there are doubts as to the extent they will enhance food security, increase crop and fish production for domestic consumption and reduce poverty.

Organised resistance to these government policies is mounting. Examples include the case of Canadian company Tiomin's bid to mine titanium on the coast of Kenya, which has been stalled now for over 10 years; the boycott of Delmonte products, which saw reforms to working practices in the firm's pineapple fields in Kenya; the advocacy by Kenyan human rights organisations against flower farms in Naivasha over unethical work practices and the use of dangerous chemicals; and now the Dominion advocacy. So far this has been grossly underestimated but in the fullness of time it will prove potent and fierce.

# TRADING FOOD RIGHTS AND GM CROPS

## INTERVIEW WITH MARIAM MAYET

June 2006

Genetically modified (GM) crops are touted by some as the answer to world hunger; by others as a dangerous intervention by multinational agribusiness that will have far-reaching impacts on all aspects of human life. Pambazuka News asked Mariam Mayet from the African Centre for Biodiversity for her views on the implications of GM crops for Africa.

**Pambazuka News:** What are the implications of GM crops for human life generally, including the human rights of populations and farmers?

**Mariam Mayet:** The risks posed by GM food are extremely contentious in current scientific discourse, primarily because the GM industry has failed, to date, to provide conclusive evidence that GM foods are safe. Amidst the enthusiasm for genetic engineering, there has been little space for critical reflection. Leaping into genetic engineering brings with it a wide range of biosafety issues including health and environmental risks, and broader socio-economic impacts. It requires the acceptance of intellectual property rights on living organisms, the privatisation of public research, and costly research and development at the expense of farmer-based innovation. Amid all the complexities of the legal and scientific arguments, decisions must be made in Africa about the measures to be taken to protect human health, agricultural biodiversity and farming systems.

**Pambazuka News:** So what decisions are being taken? Have governments introduced laws to govern this area?

**Mariam Mayet:** Very recently, the African Centre for Biodiversity did an analysis of the draft bio-safety law of Mozambique. Mozambique views genetic engineering as having a role to play in agriculture, food security and human healthcare, but believes that the risks have to be managed by the creation of an enabling legislative environment. In other words, Mozambique will follow the route taken by South Africa and permit the entry of GM crops into its agriculture systems after an evaluation of the risk assessment data provided by an applicant.

Currently, Mozambique's seed law prohibits the import and planting of GM seed. But Mozambique does accept GM food aid, including and especially from the United States of America. USAID's Food for Progress (FFP) has provided 15,500 tonnes of Public Law 480 (a US law relating to food aid) emergency food assistance valued at $11.6 million to Mozambique through the World Food Programme.[1]

Without dwelling on the politics of hunger and food aid, it is worth pointing out that the opening or maintaining of markets is a key objective of Public Law 480. This law clearly asserts that the purpose of US food aid programmes is to 'develop and expand export markets for US agricultural commodities'.[2] A position repeatedly stated by US government officials is that the opening of new markets is immensely important for the future of US agriculture.[3] Moreover, US agribusiness has been the main beneficiary of US food aid programmes.

Therefore, in considering the Mozambique law, it is worth warning that countries should not be pushed into believing that GM food aid is the only alternative to consider during emergencies. Countries should be careful when developing legislation that their laws will not subsequently be used as a conduit to push GM food aid into the rest of Africa.

**Pambazuka News:** So there are definitely some vested interests operating in the trade in GM crops. What role does the World Trade Organisation (WTO) play?

**Mariam Mayet:** The US, the world's largest producer of GM crops, has effectively used the threat of WTO sanctions against developing countries such as Sri Lanka, Bolivia, South Korea and Thailand when these countries tried to ban or restrict imports of GM crops and adopt biosafety measures.

Countries in Africa have also been the target of US-style pressure: one of the main reasons given for Egypt's initial support of the US, Argentina and Canada WTO complaint against the EU (on 13 May 2003 the US, along with Canada, Argentina and Egypt, filed a complaint in the WTO against the EU's de facto moratorium on genetically modified organisms) was that Egypt would be rewarded with a free trade agreement in 2004; an offer retracted with indecent speed when Egypt subsequently withdrew from the complaint, stating that their decision was in recognition of 'the need to preserve adequate and effective consumer and environmental protection'.[4]

Similarly, in May 2003, when Sudan banned the import of GM food aid, it was forced to issue a series of temporary waivers enabling food aid shipments to the country to continue while alternatives were found. The US response was to suspend food aid shipments to Sudan and exert enormous pressure on the government to rescind the ban. The government relented and ended up extending the waiver for six months, allowing the distribution of GM food aid to continue.

146

---

## Toxic waste in Africa

### February 2006

IN THE TOXIC WASTE trade, there's no justice for Africa's citizens and their right to a clean environment.

Africa has long been used as a dumping ground for outdated and dangerous chemicals and toxic waste. This industry is a multibillion dollar one, but Africa offers a cheap alternative: in Europe, waste disposal can cost as much as $3,000 a tonne, while in Africa is can be as little as $5, according to 'Africa waste trade'.

African governments desperate for foreign income will often accept waste from overseas, or will continue storing their own old, outdated and unused toxic waste because disposal is too costly. There are currently over 48,000 tonnes of prohibited and outdated pesticides being stored in Africa, including some of the most poisonous compounds ever made, such as DDT and chlordane says a People and Planet report entitled 'New chance to defuse Africa's toxic time-bomb'.

Further, even currently, it is estimated that 30 per cent of the pesticides sold annually in developing countries – worth $900 million in 2000 alone – fail to meet international standards, and are often mislabelled or unmarked. The responsibility to dispose of these stocks is left to Africa alone – even though the pesticides may have come from elsewhere. It is estimated that it will cost African nations $250 million to dispose of these stocks.

**Sources**
*'Africa waste trade': http://www.american.edu/TED/oauwaste.htm*
*'New chance to defuse Africa's toxic time-bomb': http://www.peopleandplanet.net/doc.php?id=1375*

---

Hence, the extent to which African countries and indeed, developing countries, will be given opportunities to take biosafety measures aimed at banning or severely restricting the trade in GM crops will be greatly influenced by the outcome of the complaint submitted during May 2003, by the United States, Canada and Argentina to the WTO, against the EU Measures Affecting the Approval and Marketing of Biotech Products (EC-Biotech).[5] For those of us in Africa, reliant on trade and aid from the US, the WTO challenge most certainly has conveyed a lasting message that either we open our markets for GM food and seeds or face reprisals.

**Pambazuka News:** You mention GM food aid. Should food aid not be welcomed?

**Mariam Mayet:** The most frequent criticism of food aid is that it impacts on local food security. Food aid acts as a disincentive to local production by driving down domestic prices. Local farmers may withdraw from producing a surplus, forcing governments to import to cover the growing deficit. Alternatively, it may lead a government to neglect its own agricultural sector, relying on aid or imports rather than facilitating local agricultural development. It may also introduce a taste for a particular food which is not produced locally, therefore undermining the long-term potential for self-sufficiency. Crucially, the provision of food aid is intimately tied to the disposal of highly subsidised surplus food to the planet's poorest and most vulnerable people.

Already, controversy over the shipment of GM food aid has twice erupted in Africa. During the Southern African food crisis in 2001/2002, Zambia imposed a ban on GM food aid, and several other Southern African countries imposed various restrictions. Last year, Angola and Sudan introduced restrictions on GM food aid. These countries are almost always presented with a false choice between accepting GM food or facing dire consequences, whereas there are almost always non-GM alternatives available nationally, regionally and internationally.

**Pambazuka News:** What has been the role of civil society in Africa? Does it have a say in any parts of the decision-making process about GM crops? Has civil society been active in opposing GM crops coming into Africa?

**Mariam Mayet:** Civil society in Africa is active – alive and kicking – but quietly. The fact that African countries (except for South Africa) have not taken any decisions on biosafety grounds to permit the commercial import and growing of GMOs is a huge victory for us. In the rest of Africa, over the last five years, only eight other countries have conducted field trials of GM crops: Burkina Faso, Egypt, Kenya, Morocco, Senegal, Tanzania, Zambia and Zimbabwe, on small plots of land.

The key target countries for USAID, the World Bank and the gene giants are the cotton markets in West Africa. However, some farmers here have already rejected GM crops. Recently, in an unprecedented move, farmers in Mali voted not to grow GM crops on their land. In a 'farmers' jury', cotton growers and other farmers debated the issue and came to the conclusion that their government should reject GM crops. The citizens' jury was hosted by the regional government (Assemblée Régionale de Sikasso) and was designed and facilitated by the London-based International Institute for Environment and Development and RIBios, the University of Geneva's Biosafety Interdisciplinary Network, together with a wide range of local partners in Mali.

**Notes**

1 USAID (2006) 'Southern Africa – food insecurity', 3 February.

2 United States Department of Agriculture, US Food Aid Programs Description: Public Law 480, Food For Progress And Section 416(B) <http://www.fas.usda.gov/excredits/pl480/pl480brief.html>.

3 Hembree Brandon (2001) 'Veneman says more farm aid likely', *Southwest Farm Press*, 21 June <http://southwestfarmpress.com/ar/farming_veneman_says_farm/>.

4 Letter from Suleiman Awaad, the Egyptian ambassador to the EU, cited in Al Amrani (2003) 'Egypt follows EU line on GM', *Middle East Times*, 6 June.
5 European Communities-Measures Affecting the Approval and Marketing of Biotech Products (EC-Biotech), WT/DS291.

# INTERNATIONAL TRADE (IN)JUSTICE
# OR THE SURVIVAL OF THE FATTEST —
# THE EFFECTS OF AGRICULTURAL SUBSIDIES

### TOPE AKINWANDE

June 2006

Trade justice, or injustice, has been on the international agenda 'like never before'. Academics and activists are campaigning for just trade and even rich countries are giving the impression that they are willing to address injustices in the global system. Tope Akinwande looks at what the reality is for West African cotton farmers.

While 70 per cent of the population of Africa work in agriculture, only a few per cent do so in rich countries. Yet rich countries support their agriculture to the tune of a staggering $279 billion a year. That's over ten times current aid to Africa. That's a sum comparable to the income of the whole of sub-Saharan Africa. Market barriers keep out developing countries that have a natural advantage in producing agricultural goods. Average tariffs between rich countries are only 3 per cent, but can rise to over 200 per cent in the US for fruits and nuts, or to 300 per cent in the EU for meat ...
Hilary Benn, UK Secretary of State for International Development[1]

During the 2005 Global Week for Action organised to campaign against trade injustice, I saw a sculpture by Jens Galschiot, a controversial Danish sculptor. Titled the 'Survival of the Fattest', the bronze sculpture depicted a very skinny man – with protruding ribs – carrying fat and well-fed Justitia, the Western goddess of justice, on his bent back. Justitia had a scale in her right hand and a long pole in her left hand on which was inscribed: 'I'm sitting on the back of a man – He is sinking under the burden – I would do anything to help him – Except stepping down from his back.'

Some people might genuinely wonder how there could be injustice in trade between two consenting people or sovereign countries who have goods to sell or exchange with one another. Since trade is not meant to be a donor–recipient relationship but one in which one country has something to sell to another to meet the needs of its populace, you might wonder how injustice could come into it or why a country could not move on to another buyer if it was not getting a good deal somewhere. If trade – as it has been simply defined by the *Cambridge International Dictionary* – is 'the activity of buying and selling, or exchanging, goods and/or services between people or countries', why should there be any injustice?

One of the most contentious issues in international politics and trade in recent times has been the issue of trade (in)justice. There have been systematic mobilisations around trade justice, particularly for Africa, like never before. Non-governmental organisations (NGOs), world leaders, academics and activists around the world are leading the campaign to ensure fair trade. In the UK, the Justice Movement, an umbrella campaign organisation of over 70 NGOs, is campaigning and lobbying the UK government in various ways for trade justice – not free trade – with compassionate rules to benefit poor people and the environment.[2]

In the face of these campaigns, richer countries have also given the impression that they are willing to redress the seeming 'trade injustice' through various world trade negotiations. These negotiations are known as 'rounds' and are named after the places where they were initiated, hence the Tokyo, Uruguay and Doha rounds. Apart

---

*The reality of international trade – like any other form of activity with vested interests to protect – is that there have been some trading practices that are deemed unfair.*

---

from these 'rounds', rich countries are apparently doing everything humanly possible (international development aid, structural adjustment policies turned poverty reduction strategy papers, the Millennium Development Goals, America's Africa Growth and Opportunity Act (AGOA) …) to eradicate (the less pretentious ones use the word 'alleviate') poverty in poor countries like Mali and Burkina Faso.

However, the reality is something else. The reality of international trade – like any other form of activity with vested interests to protect – is that there have been some trading practices that are deemed unfair. The most prominent of these 'sharp practices' is the provision of subsidies to Western farmers by their governments. These subsidies encourage farmers to produce irrespective of the market and the beauty of it all is that they are sure of a minimal income.

There are different types of agricultural subsidies. While some are directly linked to the level of production others, such as subsidies for water irrigation, are indirectly linked. Others, such as export subsidies, are used to promote exports of agricultural products. The surplus production is put on the world market which, because there is high availability of a particular commodity, can force a decrease in price. This has been happening for years in the international agricultural trade sector. Developed countries, led by the European Union (EU) and the United States (USA), significantly subsidise their agriculture, which allows their farmers and related industries to sell their products at a lower rate than the cost of production.[3]

In 2001/02, the US, Chinese, Spanish and Greek governments subsidised their cotton producers by over $6 billion dollars. US farmers alone are said to receive almost $4 billion in subsidies. US and European subsidies to domestic producers continue to impose enormous costs on poor countries. The welfare costs of the EU's Common Agricultural Policy (CAP) have been well over the development aid given to all sub-Saharan Africa.

*Since the 'international community' led by the US is aware of the predicament of African countries such as Burkina Faso and Mali, why do they continue to subsidise their domestic farmers?*

In 'Cultivating poverty: the impact of US cotton subsidies in Africa', Oxfam argues that the rock-bottom cotton price can be blamed directly on enormous subsidies paid to US cotton farmers as they are first among equals in the harvesting of subsidies. These subsidies are destroying livelihoods in Africa and other developing countries, with rural communities being the worst hit.[4]

## Killing Burkina Faso and Mali softly

The cost of cotton production in west and central Africa is very low compared to other cotton-producing countries. African cotton farmers could compete with their counterparts from developed countries if they were not enjoying the massive subsidies of their governments. This has been succinctly expressed by a West African minister who said that his country was 'happy to compete with US farmers but not with the US Treasury'.[5] Sahel countries like Burkina Faso and Mali have a comparative 'advantage'[6] in the production of cotton and the rapid increase in their productivity has shown that they could make considerable developmental gains over time.

In the 1990s, the World Bank encouraged Mali to cultivate cotton because that was its comparative advantage. The West African country threw all its energy and meagre resources into cotton production, rapidly becoming the second largest cotton producer in Africa ahead of Egypt. Despite this Malian 'success story', it could not sell its produce at reasonable rates as American producers with lower comparative advantage enjoyed a record harvest.

The only plausible reason for this bumper harvest of cotton by American farmers was the subsidies they received. It is said that 25,000 American cotton producers received US$13.9 billion between 1999 and 2005, which represents a subsidy rate of 89.5 per cent.[7] Annually, this represents about US$3.2 billion of subsidies for American cotton producers, plus US$1.6 billion in export aid.[8]

These subsidies had a disastrous effect on the Malian economy as its cotton farmers could not compete with their American counterparts. Indeed, Mali lost the equivalent of 1.7 per cent of GDP and 8 per cent of export earnings. These losses are bigger than the US$37.7 million Mali received from USAID in 2001. It is on record that the Malian finance minister at the time made this disturbing statement: 'The money that those countries put into agricultural subsidies is five times what they give as development assistance. And we've always said to rich countries, "You are hypocrites. You tell us to play the rules of open market at the same time you subsidise your farmers and kill our farmers".'[9]

Burkina Faso is one of the poorest countries in the world. Though it has significant reserves of gold, its almost non-existing industrial base has left its mining in the hands of dubious businessmen. Cotton is the mainstay for 90 per cent of Burkinabes.

According to a study carried out by WHO in Burkina Faso, the expansion of cotton farming painted a positive future for development in the country. However, continuous subvention of Western farmers has made it impossible for Burkinabe farmers to compete in the international market. Like many countries in the Sahel, Burkina Faso cannot prepare adequately for the food crises it experiences. It is perpetually locked in a vicious cycle of international aid.

This dire situation made President Blaise Compaore of Burkina Faso, a rather shrewd talker and 'great friend of the West', cry out recently in frustration that: 'Several central and west African countries are victims of injustice by the US and EU. These countries subsidise their agricultural producers, ignoring the rules of WTO. Such practices are undermining the fragile national economies of countries that depend on cotton.'[10] This situation is not peculiar to these two countries. It is the same for many African countries whose economies are mainly agricultural based.

When signing the US Farm Bill in May 2002, President George Bush made a very revealing statement about his choices concerning international agricultural trade:

> I told the people, I said if you give me a chance to be President, we are not going to treat our agricultural industry as a secondary citizen when it comes to opening markets. And I mean that … The farm bill is important legislation … It will promote farmer independence, and preserve the farm way of life. It helps America's farmers and therefore it helps America.[11]

This agricultural bill, which sharply increased subsidies and protections for US producers, was passed while the 'international community' was pushing for a Doha round of trade talks that would deal with agriculture.

Since the 'international community' led by the US is aware of the predicament of African countries such as Burkina Faso and Mali, why do they continue to subsidise their domestic farmers? Why cannot the US stop subsidising its farmers and allow poor countries like Mali to earn a decent income and stop 'pan-handling', year in, year out, for development aid? Why are the rich countries advocating free trade and open markets in developing countries while European and US subsidies to their farmers are destroying markets for vulnerable farmers in sub-Saharan Africa?

The answer is easy and lies in the 'national interest' of Western countries. Much as the notion of 'national interest' is a shifting one, it reveals the true motives of powerful world leaders. It also guards us against two popular misconceptions about the determination of a state's foreign policy – the motives of leaders and ideological preferences.

While political leaders will cast their policies in ideological terms (free trade, democracy, human rights, justice, etc), they are inevitably confronted by what is desirable and what is possible. There is no room for moral or ethical concerns, prejudice, political philosophy or individual preference in the determination of foreign policy because actions are constrained by the interests of the state and its power to enforce them. The 'national interest', which ought to be the sole pursuit of political leadership, is always defined in terms of strategic and economic capability.

## Conclusion

In international politics, no government will risk its national interest, whatever it happens to be at any given time. It is 'sacrosanct' for the survival of the nation.

In the light of this basic reality, the EU and US will continue to protect their farmers as long as it is politically expedient. This is not an issue of justice or injustice. It is simply that the survival of their states (and the political ambitions of their leaders) requires the protection of their 'national interests', of which subsidies to domestic farmers are just one part. If that cannot be achieved, then these leaders would be considered incompetent or forced to leave.

The onus is on the governments at the receiving end of these 'sharp' trade practices to raise their game and find a strong negotiating platform. It is not going to be easy, as we have seen with Brazil and the WTO saga. It is either for these countries, and those who are campaigning along with them for fair trade, to find a way of putting fat Justitia down in order to have serious negotiations or to carry her on their bent backs for a long time to come. Nothing can be more certain than that Justitia will not want to get off the back of the skinny man for as long as it is possible. Who would, except when compassion for others surpasses passion for self?

154

**Notes**

1 Hilary Benn (2005) 'How can we get trade justice?', a speech delivered at the London School of Economics, 29 June <http://www.dfid.gov.uk/news/files>.

2 See the Trade Justice Movement website <http://www.tjm.org.uk>.

3 Nigel Grimwade (1996) *International Trade Policy – A Contemporary Analysis*. London: Routledge.

4 Kevin Watkins (2002) 'Cultivating poverty: the impact of US cotton subsidies in Africa', *Oxfam Briefing Paper* 30, Oxfam International <http://www.oxfam.org.uk/what_we_do/issues/trade/downloads/bp30-cotton.pdf>.

5 Benn (2005).

6 Comparative advantage is what a country can produce with less cost at less time and effort above other countries.

7 See http://www.lwf-humanrights.org/issues.php.

8 Ibid.

9 See Watkins (2002).

10 Ibid.

11 See http://www.whitehouse.gov/news/releases/2002/08/20020806-4.html-45.

# SACRIFICING THE RIGHT TO FOOD
# ON THE ALTAR OF FREE TRADE

**JAGJIT PLAHE**

January 2007

The right to food versus international trade commitments – that's the balance that developing countries have to strike in a globalised world. Increasingly it's the food security of their populations that is being sacrificed, with developing countries having to negotiate the right to food within the World Trade Organisation, says Jagjit Plahe. 'How, when and if states can regulate trade to uphold the right to food will be determined by international trade rules, and not by international human rights standards,' she states.

## Food security in a human rights framework

Food security[1] is a 'multifaceted concept, variously defined and interpreted'.[2] The World Bank,[3] for example, defines food security as: 'access by all people at all times to sufficient food, in terms of quality, quantity, and diversity for an active and healthy life without risk of loss of that access.'

The United Nations Committee on Economic, Social and Cultural Rights goes a step further and defines food security in the context of the human right to food. The right to food means that it is both available and accessible. According to the committee the availability of food constitutes the 'quantity and quality sufficient to satisfy the dietary needs of individuals' and therefore 'refers to the possibility of feeding oneself directly from production land or other natural resources, or from well-functioning distribution, processing and market systems that can provide more food from the site of production to where it is needed'.[4] Importantly, the definition focuses on the role of the state in ensuring food security. As Zhang notes:

> International human rights law imposes upon States obligations to respect, protect and fulfil this right, like any other basic human right. Thus, to ensure food security is in fact the implementation of obligations under international human rights law.[5]

The Food and Agricultural Organisation[6] estimates that 842 million people in the world are undernourished, of whom 798 million people are from the third world. Developing countries therefore have a mammoth task at hand to address food insecurity. These countries, however, also have the responsibility to uphold their obligations under international trade law. Currently, 15 out of the 20 countries which are chronically food insecure (where over 35 per cent of the population is food insecure) are members of the WTO. Similarly, 24 out of 28 food insecure countries, where between 20 and 34 per cent of the population is food insecure, are also members of the World Trade Organisation. These states have to undertake a precarious balancing act between their various obligations under international law. Their options for addressing food security are seriously limited by their obligations under the WTO Agreement on Agriculture (AoA).

## The notion of food security in the AoA

The *raison d'etre* of the AoA is to liberalise global trade in agriculture. The AoA's stated long-term objective is 'to provide for substantial progressive reductions on agricultural support and protection sustained over an agreed period of time, resulting in correcting and preventing restrictions and distortions in world agricultural markets'.[7] The neo-classical assumption behind this objective is that the market will address problems of food security. These assumptions are well stated in various WTO documents.

> *The neo-classical assumption behind the objective of the WTO's Agreement on Agriculture is that the market will address problems of food security.*

The 1986 GATT Punta del Este Declaration, for example, which set out the negotiation objectives of the Uruguay round, starts off by asserting that GATT contracting parties are: 'Determined to develop a more open, viable and durable multilateral trading system' and that they are 'convinced that such action would promote growth and development'.[8]

Supporters of the AoA argue that liberalised trade in agriculture will enhance food security since global resources will be allocated more efficiently. Using the theories of comparative advantage and factor endowments,[9] they argue 'that the differences in productivity and opportunity costs of production between countries' are the main reasons why countries should engage in international trade.[10] They contend that free market conditions will create win-win situations for all, and 'those [countries] that gain from trade [can] fully compensate those that lose, and still be better off: the total gain will be better than the total loss'.[11]

One of the objectives of the Punte Del Este Declaration clearly reflects this view, stating that negotiations will 'bring about further liberalisation and expansion of world trade to the benefit of all countries, especially less-developed contracting parties'.[12]

In supporting free market conditions, the AoA seeks to reduce the role of the state in agricultural production and trade. This has both direct and indirect implications for food security, particularly in developing countries where agriculture plays such a vital role in the national economy. Agriculture accounts for over 50 per cent of total employment in the third world. In food insecure countries, however, the role of agriculture is far more critical, comprising 30 per cent of GDP and employing nearly two-thirds of the work force.[13]

The AoA therefore has extremely profound and far-reaching implications for developing countries. These implications have brought to the fore an intense and bitterly divisive debate on the roles and responsibilities of the state in a globalising era. As well as being ideological, the debate is also based on some very specific structural problems with the AoA, which have had the effect of allowing developed countries not only to continue to protect their agricultural sectors, but ironically, to increase their protection. Critics of the AoA therefore argue that far from achieving food security, the AoA has had the opposite effect.[14, 15, 16, 17, 18] This is not only due to the simplistic ideological assumptions which underpin the agreement, but also because the agreement legitimises and perpetuates an imbalance in world agricultural trade which prevents developing countries' agricultural sectors from growing in the way that is necessary for improved food security.

## The food security implications of the AoA

Given the human rights definition of the right to food, nation states have an obligation to protect the livelihoods of small farmers, enabling them to produce food for their local community and ensuring that they gain a fair share in the commodity chain if they are engaged in production for the export market. Also, the state should have the right to protect the livelihoods of small farmers who suffer from cheap agricultural imports. The AoA, however, curtails the freedom of nation states to protect food security.

The neo-classical model, which underpins the AoA, assumes that all countries will be better off under free trade. The model, however, ignores several key elements of the economics of international agriculture. First, it does not address the reality of declining terms of trade (the ratio of export prices to the ratio of import prices) for primary products. Countries that are chronically food insecure primarily export raw materials which increasingly face declining terms of trade in the world market;[15] the products they export fetch a much lower price in the world market relative to the price of their imports. Moreover, unprocessed commodities such as sugar, tea, coffee and cocoa beans constitute a very small portion of the overall price of chocolates, sweet biscuits, processed tea and coffee. In many cases, farmers engaged in the production of primary products for export are simply price takers and have not shared in the big gains which have taken place in global markets.[16]

---

*How, when and if states can regulate trade to uphold the right to food will be determined by international trade rules, and not by international human rights standards.*

---

Second, the model assumes that 'buyers and sellers in different markets meet each other as independent agents, in which no single buyer or seller has a monopoly'[17] and that a reduction in trade barriers will lead to more opportunities for all potential buyers and sellers.

Freer trade does not automatically lead to market access. The integration of producers and exporters in developing countries is carefully 'managed' by lead firms.[18] These lead firms are often huge multinational corporations based in the OECD countries, and they wield immense power over agricultural commodity chains. The liberalisation of agricultural markets does not benefit all agents in commodity chains equally, especially those that are locked in at the production stage. The existing literature on the governance of commodity chains in the current era of globalisation does not point to 'equal gains for all'. In fact, some coffee, cocoa, horticultural and fruit farmers from developing countries in Latin America and Africa, have steadily become poorer, or have lost their livelihoods altogether, because of the concentration in agents further downstream – branded merchandisers, international traders and supermarkets – and due to structural adjustment and deregulation of agriculture in their own countries.[19]

Third, the model assumes that the global market is competitive. However, the reality is that agriculture is the most highly protected sector in international trade, with the OECD countries subsidising their domestic production by US$1 billion a day. High subsidies in rich countries – which have led to dumping in the world market – threaten small farmers in poor countries and hamper their exports.

## The AoA does not discourage dumping

Dumping is defined as the sale of products in the global market at less than the cost of production. Dumped agricultural produce in world markets leads to the widespread displacement of farmers from their own markets in the developing world, because they cannot compete with highly subsidised products.[20] These farmers lose their livelihoods and become food insecure. Also, farmers in developing countries who are engaged in production for the export market suffer from severely depressed prices, due to the high levels of dumping in the world market. Various studies outline the complex implications of domestic and export subsidies in OECD countries.[21]

One of the main implications of the AoA for food security is that it has not curtailed the high levels of trade distorting protection given to agricultural producers in the OECD countries and therefore it has not curbed dumping in international markets. This is because the baseline periods chosen under the AoA (1986–88, which was the time from when agricultural support had to be reduced) was a time when 'trade distorting' domestic and export support was historically high in the OECD countries.[22]

Also, there were no reductions in commitments for domestic subsidies, which are deemed to be 'minimally trade distorting' under the AoA, a term which remains undefined. As the OECD contends, 'it is virtually impossible for domestic support measures to be fully de-linked from production and trade and therefore nondistortionary'.[23]

The EU alone spends US$120 billion a year on domestic support.[24] The high subsidies allow the EU and the US to dump agricultural produce in world markets.

---

*Dumping is defined as the sale of products in the global market at less than the cost of production. Dumped agricultural produce in world markets leads to the widespread displacement of farmers from their own markets in the developing world, because they cannot compete with highly subsidised products.*

---

According to Oxfam,[25] half of the world's maize is exported by the US alone. However, the US export prices are one-fifth below the cost of production. Similarly, the EU is the largest exporter of white sugar, and the EU export price of sugar is one-quarter of the actual production cost. Approximately 60 per cent of domestic agricultural support in OECD countries is exempt from domestic support commitments under the AoA.[26] The three major users of domestic support – the EU, the US and Japan – have met their AoA requirements despite the fact that domestic support has in fact increased in these countries since 1995, when the AoA came into effect.

The proposed changes – under the Doha round of negotiations – to the domestic support pillar do not address the flawed structure of the AoA or the simplistic assumptions of the neoliberal model on which the AoA is based. The categories of domestic support (trade distorting and non-trade distorting) are still maintained, despite the fact that domestic support has actually increased in the post-Uruguay round era. With these categories still in place, it is quite unlikely that the proposed changes will have any far-reaching implications in terms of dumping. Ironically, one of the main ways in which developing countries can protect their own markets from dumped products is through the use of tariffs. However, they no longer have the automatic right to use tariffs to address dumping: while AoA rules make room for dumping, they prevent developing countries' use of tariffs.

*According to Oxfam, half of the world's maize is exported by the US alone. However, the US export prices are one-fifth below the cost of production. Similarly, the EU is the largest exporter of white sugar, and the EU export price of sugar is one-quarter of the actual production cost.*

## Curtailed use of tariffs

Tariffs are the most viable tool available to developing countries to protect their markets from price volatility and from sudden increases in imports. The market access rules of the WTO require all members to reduce both tariff and non-tariff barriers. In the current round of negotiations, developing countries have argued for special safeguard mechanisms as well as provisions for special products, which would be exempt from reduction commitments. While this approach has not been rejected outright by the OECD countries, the fact is that developing countries no longer have the freedom to pursue policies to protect food security. In order to uphold their human rights obligations developing countries now have to negotiate this right within the WTO.

## Conclusion

In the current era of globalisation, developing countries are struggling to uphold both their internationally recognised human rights and international trade obligations. In terms of food security, the WTO's AoA does not acknowledge nation states' food security obligations or needs. A state can no longer automatically take measures to protect the right to food, but must negotiate for this right at the WTO. How, when and if states can regulate trade to uphold the right to food will be determined by international trade rules, and not by international human rights standards. The right to food should be fundamental. However, in this era of liberalised trade, it has been compromised.

**Notes**

1 The terms food security and the right to food are used interchangeably in this paper.

2 Food and Agricultural Organisation (FAO) (2003a) *Trade Reforms and Food Security: Conceptualising the Linkages*. Rome: Food and Agriculture Organisation of the United Nations, p. 3.

3 World Bank (1986) *Poverty and Hunger: Issues and Options for Food Security in Developing Countries*. Washington, DC: World Bank.

4 United Nations Committee on Economic, Social and Cultural Rights (1999) 'Substantive, issues arising in the implementation of the international covenant on economic, social and cultural rights: General comment 12: The right to adequate food', E/C.12/1999/5, United Nations, Geneva.

5 Zhang, R. (2004) 'Food security: food trade regime and food aid regime', *Journal of International Economic Law*, 7(3): p. 567.

6 Food and Agriculture Organisation (FAO) (2003b) *The State of Food Insecurity in the World, 2003, Monitoring Progress towards the World Food Summit and Millennium Development Goals*. Rome: FAO.

7 World Trade Organisation (WTO) (1995) *The Results of the Uruguay Round*. Geneva: World Trade Organisation.

8 General Agreement on Tariffs and Trade (GATT) (1986) 'Punta Del Este Declaration, Ministerial Declaration of 20 September 1986'. GATT: Geneva.

9 Factor endowments or Heckscher-Ohlin (HO) is the leading theory on what determines a given country's trade pattern. The theory was first developed by Swedish economic historian Eli Heckscher and later by his student Bertil Ohlin. According to Ohlin, 'Commodities requiring for their production much of [abundant factors of production] and little of [scarce factors] are exported in exchange of goods that call for factors in the opposite proportions.' Thus indirectly, factors in abundant supply are exported and factors in scanty supply are imported.

10 FAO (2003a) p. 13.

11 FAO (2003a) p. 14.

12 GATT (1986).

13 FAO (2003b) p. 16.

14 Murphy, S. (2002) *Managing the Invisible Hand, Markets, Farmers and International Trade*, Institute for Agriculture and Trade Policy; Oxfam (2005) 'Kicking down the door: how upcoming WTO talks threaten farmers in poor countries', Oxfam Briefing Paper, 72; IATP (2005) 'Planting the rights seed: A human rights perspective on agriculture trade and the WTO', Backgrounder 1 in the THREAD series; Bernal, L. E. (2003) 'The WTO agriculture negotiations and developing countries', a background paper on the occasion of the 5th WTO ministerial conference in Cancun, Mexico, 10–14 September, CIDSE; Stevens, C., Greenhill, R., Kennan, J. and Devereux S. (2002) 'The WTO Agreement on Agriculture and Food Security', Commonwealth Secretariat.

15 Importantly, the AoA does not address tariff escalation (where higher levels of tariffs are applied to higher levels of production) in the OECD countries, which actually discourages developing countries from investing in value added activities.

16 MacEwan, A. (1999) *Neo-liberalism or Democracy*, Zed Books, New York, p. 53.

17 Kanji, N. and Barrientos, S. (2002) 'Trade liberalisation, poverty and livelihoods: understanding the

linkages', *IDS Working Paper* 159, Institute of Development Studies, Brighton, Sussex, p. 19.

18 Humphrey, J. and Schmitz, H. (2001) 'Governance in global value chains', *IDS Bulletin*, 32(3).

19 Gwynne, R. N. (1999) 'Globalisation, commodity chains and fruit exporting regions in Chile', *Royal Dutch Geographical Society*, 90(2): 211–25; Dolan, C., Humphrey, J. and Harris-Pascal, C. (1999) 'Horticulture commodity chains: the impact of the UK market on the African fresh vegetable industry', IDS Working Paper 96, Institute of Development Studies, University of Sussex, Sussex; Fold, N. (2001) 'Restructuring of the European chocolate industry and its impacts on cocoa production in West Africa', Journal of Economic Geography, 1(4): 405–20; Ponte, S. (2001) 'The latte revolution? Winners and losers in the restructuring of the global coffee marketing chain', Centre for Development Research, Copenhagen; Ponte, S. (2002) 'Brewing a bitter cup? Deregulation, quality and the re-organization of coffee marketing in East Africa', Journal of Agrarian Change, 2(2): 248–72.

20 Bernal (2003); IATP (2005).

21 Beierle, T. C. (2002) 'From Uruguay to Doha: agricultural trade negotiations at the World Trade Organisation', *Discussion Paper* 02-13, Resources for the Future, Washington DC; Matthews, A. (2000) 'Multilateral trade reform in agriculture and the developing countries', Trinity Economic Paper Series, 2000/10; Matthews, A. (2001) 'Developing countries' position in WTO agricultural trade negotiations', Development Policy Review, 20(1): pp. 75–90; Organisation of Economic Cooperation and Development (OECD) (2001a) Agricultural Policies in OECD Countries: Monitoring and Evaluation, Highlights. Paris: OECD; OECD (2001b) The Uruguay Round Agreement on Agriculture: An Evaluation of Its Implementation in OECD Countries. Paris: OECD; Murphy (2002); Diaz-Bonilla, E., Robinson, S., Thomas, M. and Yanoma, Y. (2002), WTO, Agriculture and Developing Countries: A Survey of Issues. Washington DC: International Food Policy Research Institute; Oxfam (2002) 'Boxing match in agricultural trade: will WTO negotiations knock out the world's poorest farmers?' *Oxfam Briefing Paper* 32; Oxfam (2005) 'Kicking down the door: how upcoming WTO talks threaten farmers in poor countries', *Oxfam Briefing Paper* 72.

22 Beierle (2002), 33. In addition, the formula to reduce trade-distorting support was calculated on an aggregated basis, rather than a commodity-by-commodity basis. This allows developed countries to continue to provide much higher support to sensitive commodities and still stay within the AoA limits, according to Mathews (2001, p. 82).

23 OECD (2001a) pp. 63 and 64.

24 Beierle (2002), 30.

25 Oxfam (2002), p. 17.

26 Oxfam (2002) p. 18.

# EUROPE – THE 'PROMISED LAND'
# FOR AFRICA'S UNEMPLOYED

**TOPE AKINWANDE**

January 2007

The summer of 2006 saw a surge in immigration to mainland Europe from some African countries. While European leaders are attempting to stop the wave, Tope Akinwande points to the hypocrisy of the massive farm subsidies received by European farmers and the trade policies that make it impossible for African agriculture sectors to survive.

Like all humans, Africans have migrated since the dawn of history. They have moved for demographic, economic and political reasons.[1] In recent times, there has been a spotlight on African immigration to European countries. As the legal requirements for entry into Europe become stricter and more cumbersome and as opportunities to make a decent livelihood shrink in sub-Saharan Africa, its people have resorted to desperate means in order to gain access to what is generally considered to be the 'Promised Land' for many Africans outside Europe. This has been ever more apparent in West Africa, where young people travel through deserts, stowaway in ships, and try all sorts of means to reach Europe.

How did this situation arise? In the 1960s and the beginning of the 1970s, Africa's future looked bright. It was the post-independence era of 'self-determination', laden with all sorts of opportunities; almost all of the agricultural-based African economies could meet the needs of their people. An average African had no cause to risk their life by travelling in a desperate fashion to Europe when their basic needs could be met in their country of origin.

Africans who ventured to Europe for further studies were in a hurry to return home as prestigious and lucrative jobs with all the accompanying benefits awaited them. Afterwards, they only travelled to the Western world for business and leisure. The few African students who stayed in Europe were considered to be failures who could not find their feet back home.

However, things have taken a dramatic turn for the worse. Africans and especially West Africans – probably because of their coastline's proximity to Europe – are the new 'boat people', fleeing abject poverty occasioned by lack of opportunities in their countries of origin. They are constantly in the international spotlight either being rescued by European coast guards, attended to by tourists or, occasionally, having their bloated bodies washed to shore.

In the summer of 2006 – summer is said to be the preferred time to travel as the sea is supposedly calmer – it was almost a daily occurrence to see demeaning images of tired and hopeless-looking African men and women rescued by European coastguards after risking their lives to get to the Spanish Canary Islands. They used makeshift boats to negotiate the treacherous waves of the Mediterranean sea in an attempt to escape poverty back home.[2]

According to the International Organisation for Migration (IOM) and the United Nations Office for the Coordination of Humanitarian Affairs, in 2006 over 27,000 illegal immigrants turned up on the Canary Islands off the West African coast.

While the rescued sojourners are considered to be 'fortunate' to have stepped onto the shores of Europe despite the excruciating difficulties awaiting them, many Africans are not lucky enough to be intercepted mid-sea by coastguards. They perish with their desperate dreams. In 2006, the Spanish coastguard accounted for 500 bodies found in the ocean around the Canaries.

## Origin of the problem

Compared to the 1960s and early 1970s, Africa's growth in the 1980s and 1990s has been very bad. The 1980s have been described as a 'lost decade,[3] while the children of that era and the 1990s have been famously tagged the 'wasted generation' by the Nigerian Nobel Laureate, Wole Soyinka.

Despite the strong belief held by many Africa analysts that the economic woes of Africa are rooted in its 'largely documented history' of colonialism which culminated in a façade called 'independence' and the Cold War which institutionalised despotism, kleptocracy, and big-man politics, the structural adjustment programmes (SAPs) imposed by the World Bank and International Monetary Fund (IMF) have made it impossible for African countries to meet the basic needs of their people.

---

*In the summer of 2006 it was almost a daily occurrence to see demeaning images of tired and hopeless-looking African men and women rescued by European coastguards after risking their lives to get to the Canary Islands.*

---

Introduced in the 1970s to galvanise the economies of African countries following the decline in the prices of agricultural products, SAPs came with tough conditions such as privatisation, wage freezes, the elimination of price controls and the lifting of trade barriers. Instead of encouraging economic development, SAPs created a new phenomenon of heavily indebted poor countries (HIPC) which could not meet the basic needs of their people.

In its 22 June 2006 edition *The Economist*, in its characteristically sanctimonious manner, posited that 'rich countries have been generous lately, with extra aid and debt relief, giving many struggling economies a breath of air. By the end of last year,

---

*In the 1960s and the beginning of the 1970s, Africa's future looked bright. An average African had no cause to risk their life by travelling in a desperate fashion to Europe when their basic needs could be met in their country of origin.*

---

29 countries, 25 of them in Africa, had had their debt burden eased...' The magazine went on to wonder if '...Africa, often dubbed the hopeless continent, (is) finally taking off?'[4] For once, a magazine that has carelessly dubbed Africa as a 'hopeless continent' conceded that 'Africa itself deserves the credit for the upswing of its economy in the past year'.[5]

Like most of its counterparts in the international media, what *The Economist* failed to acknowledge is that the dividends of the so-called debt relief are easily drowned by one phenomenon – the international trade policies of the 'generous' industrial nations it was talking about. The debt relief issue is like giving something out with the left hand and taking it back with the right.

In March 2005, the British government, which has been in the forefront of the highly indebted poor countries initiative (HIPCI), published a detailed report of the £1.7 billion it gave to agricultural companies as subsidies. At the same time, the US – though planning to reduce its subsidies to American farmers by 5 per cent – gave about $9 billion.[6]

How on earth can African farmers compete with their European and American counterparts on the world food market? Would African governments whose national budgets are sometimes smaller than the subsidies Western farmers receive be able to subsidise their farmers to 'even the score'? They will have to face incessant unrest at home while the rest of their citizens 'hit the road' or set off for European coasts.

Oumar Hamadoun Dicko, foreign affairs minister of Mali, could not have been more precise about the causes of the recent wave of immigration of West Africans: 'Immigration is going to continue unless we address fundamental issues like the unequal terms of trade,' he said. 'African farmers can't compete and are out of world markets,' he con-cluded in a recent interview with the UN Office for the Coordination of Humanitarian Affairs.[7] He surely knows what he is talking about since Mali's cotton farmers have been greatly affected by the subsidies enjoyed by their Western counterparts.

According to the Malian Foreign Affairs Ministry, 4 million, or over a third of Mali's 11.7 million people, are currently out of the country.[8] It is noteworthy that the major-ity of these Malian emigrants are from Kayes, the main cotton-producing area of the country. They have had to leave their cotton farms to try their luck in Europe.

Money remitted by this large Malian diaspora has been vital in meeting the needs that the government has been unable to meet. Many Malians in the diaspora are building schools, dispensaries, and other amenities in their home areas. The Malian Ministry of Foreign Affairs concedes that annual Malian diaspora remittances exceed US$200 million, which is more than half of the country's export earnings.

While there has been much talk about agricultural subsidies being the main interna-tional trade policy that has hampered trade and development in Africa, it is interesting to know that there are many other types of subsidies, such as that given to the fishing industry, which have not made life easier for developing countries.

Recently, the World Wide Fund for Nature (WWF) accused Japan of paying the highest subsidies to its national fishing industry at US$2 billion. The report also indi-cated that the 15-member European Union, China, and the United States have become leading underwriters.[9] These governments give their farmers and fishing companies subsidies in the form of grants, loans and loan guarantees, equity infusions, tax prefer-ences, and price or income support.

Thiaroye-Sur-Mer is a fishing town a few kilometres from Dakar, the capital of Senegal. A few years ago and up till the end of 2005, one could see hundreds of fisher-men – both young and old – selling fish to locals and large-scale buyers from Dakar and elsewhere. Today, Thiaroye-Sur-Mer has almost become a ghost town as most of the younger fishermen have taken to the seas; this time not to fish but to try their luck in Spain's Canary Islands. They sold their means of livelihood (boats, fishing nets, etc) and bought a one-way ticket on a boat to a supposed better future in Europe.

Like many sub-Saharan African countries, Senegal has been going through an excruciating SAP that has completely destroyed its economy. Its main source of income – groundnuts – no longer fetch a good price on the international market as many substitutes have been developed. Senegal's fishing industry is losing its momentum as the country has been inundated with subsidised food, including fish from Europe and Asia, making it impossible for local fishermen to sell their catch at a decent rate and meet the basic needs of their families. The only way for these young Senegalese fishermen to survive and support their families is by trying their luck in Europe. This has become a way of life in a country where the money remitted by the Senegalese diaspora sometimes accounts for 90 per cent of income in many households.

## Which way forward?

With the recent wave of immigration to the Canary Islands, European governments, led by Spain, have been trying to curb the immigration of Africans who are willing to risk their lives to reach Europe at all costs.

The incidents of September and October 2005 where Spanish coast guards opened fire on ill-equipped boats full of African immigrants led to the adoption of the 'Rabat Declaration' on 11 July 2006 by 57 European and African countries. The declaration enjoined the 57 signatory countries to set up an action plan that would get to the core of the problem.

In September 2006, the European Union promised to provide Mali with US$542 million over five years to control the emigration of its citizens. Mali is expected to use the

---

*The Malian Ministry of Foreign Affairs concedes that annual Malian diaspora remittances exceed US$200 million, which is more than half of the country's export earnings.*

---

money to start projects aimed at discouraging young people from emigrating.

International NGOs are also trying to encourage young Africans to stay back in their countries. For example, the Spanish Red Cross has embarked on an awareness campaign in Senegal to demystify the notion of success attached to emigration. They are emphasising the harsh realities.

In addition, African celebrities have thrown themselves into the fray. One of the most successful African singers, Senegalese Youssou N'Dour is lending his fame and voice to the anti-emigration campaign. In collaboration with IOM and other well-known Senegalese musicians, he has recorded a single titled 'Emigration' where he enjoins young people not to abandon their country. One thing missing from this beautiful record is that Youssou N'Dour forgets to suggest any alternatives to Senegalese and African youths.

Can these initiatives work? Since the ones mentioned above, there have been cases of African boat people arriving in Spain and as recently as September 2006 in Malta, thus exasperating the government of the tiny country, which has just joined the European Union.

As one route is blocked, Africans perfect their 'travelling techniques'. On 20 November 2006 the Europa press agency reported how 1,293 West Africans, braving a very harsh winter, arrived in the Canary Islands, many of them in well-built fishing vessels. They also travelled with enough provisions (food, winter clothing, etc) to see them through their journey of death. Interestingly, some immigrants have gone back to the old routes, probably thinking that immigration authorities will have shifted their focus elsewhere.

## Conclusion

As I had indicated earlier, there are numerous initiatives to curb illegal immigration with the latest one being the first Ministerial Conference on Migration and Development between the EU and the entire African continent in November 2006. One of the expected outcomes of the Conference was the establishment of a framework for a joint collaboration between Europe and Africa to curb illegal immigration. The framework will consider major causes of immigration such as economic integration and development.

When one considers the impact of the remittances made by African immigrants – both legal and illegal – to their national economies and how it is, sadly, boasted of and applauded as an alternative to foreign earnings, it is difficult not to wonder if African politicians are really sincere in curbing the flow of their citizens to the West. Why should they bother when the emigration of their citizens 'relieves' them of the headache of finding the funds to embark on development projects such as building schools, hospitals and roads? If they genuinely work towards stopping them from emigrating, what alternatives do they have for farmers who cannot sell their produce? Have they got any opportunities to offer the young graduates and school leavers that are churned out in their millions into joblessness and despair?

It is noteworthy that while African politicians are silently grateful for the 'subsidies' they get from their citizens in the diaspora, Western politicians are also not keen to stop the subsidies they give to their citizens because the national interest and, in particular, their political survival depends on keeping their farmers and citizens happy.

As long as this political deadlock remains unbroken, the West and Europe in particular should be prepared to receive more and more people.

**Notes**

1 Adepoju, Aderanti (2005) *Creating a Borderless West Africa: Constraints and Prospects for Intra-Regional Migration.* UNESCO: Paris, p. 12.

2 Adepoju (2005).

3 Oshikoya, T. and Mlambo, K. (1999) in S. Kayizzi-Mugerwa (ed) *The African Economy: Policy, Institutions and the Future.* London and New York: Routledge, p. 33.

4 *The Economist* (2006) 'Africa's economy: a glimmer of light at last?', 22 June, p.24.

5 *The Economist* (2006).

6 *The Guardian* (2005) Editorial, 23 March, p. 8.

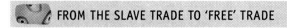

FROM THE SLAVE TRADE TO 'FREE' TRADE

7 See <www.irinnews.org> for full interview.

8 See <www.irinnews.org> for full interview.

9 See <www.wwf.org> for full report.

170

Printed in the United Kingdom
by Lightning Source UK Ltd.
124372UK00001B/27-40/A